First published in Great Britain 1985 by Colour Library Books Ltd.
CLB 1122
© 1985 Illustrations and text: Colour Library Books Ltd.,
   Guildford, Surrey, England.
Display and text filmsetting by Acesetters Ltd.,
   Richmond, Surrey, England.
Printed and bound in Barcelona Spain
Edited by Anne D. Ager.
Stylist: Pat Bailey.
Coordination: Hanni Edmonds.
ISBN 0 86283 297 7

Text by
Beverley Piper

Photography by
Peter Barry

Designed by
Philip Clucas

Produced by
Ted Smart and Gerald Hughes

Editorial Direction
David Gibbon

MICROWAVE
COOKING

BHS

Contents

Introduction

The microwave oven is one of the most exciting kitchen appliances available. It may be used to defrost, reheat, and cook foods, and is therefore more versatile than a conventional oven; in fact it can cope with 75% of your normal cooking chores.

The theory behind microwave cooking must be learned and fully understood before a microwave oven can be used to its full extent. It is a very different method of cooking, which is clean, quick, efficient, labour saving and economical.

The Principles of Microwave Cookery

The oven is plugged in by means of a 13 amp plug to a normal electrical socket and it is usually positioned on the kitchen work top. Electricity is converted into microwave energy inside the oven by the magnetron. The 'microwaves' are transferred into the oven cavity where they bounce off the metal interior and penetrate the outer 2-4cm (1"-1½") of the food. They pass through non-metal containers as though they were not there, and simply cause the molecules in the food to vibrate very fast indeed. The heat that is created passes by conduction through to the centre of the food and the food is cooked by friction heat. As a rough guide, cooking times by the microwave method are about ⅓ to ¼ of the conventional times.

Different Types of Microwave Ovens

A microwave oven may be either free standing or built-in. If built-in, it is placed in a housing unit, with a conventional oven situated above or below the microwave.

Convected Hot Air and Microwave Combined

These ovens are now widely available. They are more expensive than an ordinary microwave oven as they combine two units in one. The most common criticism of food cooked in a microwave is that it does not appear 'brown'. This is because there is no dry heat available to caramelise or 'brown' the food. Some people prefer to buy the combination ovens, which use traditional cooking methods and

microwave cooking combined. In some models both cooking methods may be used simultaneously, whilst in others the microwave and the hot air ovens are used one after the other.

Grills
Some microwave ovens offer a browning grill.

Safety
All microwave ovens offered for sale in this country pass rigorous safety tests. Choose one which has the British Standard kite mark. Microwaves are similar to radio and television waves and cannot damage body tissue.

The Output of the Microwave
The cooking time for each dish/recipe is governed by the electrical output of the microwave oven, and the output also controls the running costs of the appliance. The output is measured in watts. A 700w microwave oven (the most powerful available on the domestic market) consumes about 1.3k per hour and is, therefore, a most economical method of cooking. Microwave ovens are available with maximum power ratings of 700w, 650w, 600w and 500w. The cooking, re-heating and defrosting times vary according to the output. A 1.5kg (3lb) chicken takes 21 minutes in a 700w microwave and 28 minutes in a 500w. There is no pre-heating before use, and no cooling down after cooking.

Versatility
A microwave oven may be used to defrost, cook and reheat food. It is also well suited to the many different methods of cooking – a microwave oven can poach, shallow fat fry, braise, roast, boil and bake. It will even dry herbs for winter use, and may be used to sterilise jam jars. The oven and cooking containers stay cool, and microwave ovens are, therefore, perfectly safe for elderly people to use, and for households where there are children.

Cleaning

As the oven cabinet does not get very hot, all that is necessary is a wipe with a clean dish cloth. Should smells cling e.g. curry or fish, simply squeeze a lemon into 450ml (¾ pint) water and bring to the boil. Wipe the oven with the acidulated water. Food does not bake onto the containers so they are easier to wash up.

Turntables

Manufacturers choose different methods of ensuring that the food cooks evenly. Go by personal recommendation wherever possible. Hidden turntables are popular as they do not restrict the shape of dish used. Some ovens offer stirrer fans and turntables.

Standing Times

Standing, or equalising, time is simply the time that the food takes to finish cooking. The heat is passed from the outside to the centre by conduction. The standing time will vary according to the size and density of the food. Standing time may take place either inside or outside the microwave oven; it is an important part of microwave cookery which must be used. It is just as important after defrosting.

Containers for Use in the Microwave Oven

Special containers are available for microwave cookery, but they are not essential. The heat is localised in the food, and not in the container, so the dish itself does not usually become hot. Some plastics, Pyrex, china, glass, and even paper and basketware, may be used. Be guided by the length of time the food is to be in the microwave, and by the temperature that it will reach.

Plastic cling film is a boon to the microwave owner, as it may be used in place of a lid to cover foods and prevent splashing. Do remember to pierce cling film and roasta bags to allow steam to escape.

Metal – including tin foil – may damage the heart of the microwave oven, the magnetron, and should not be used unless specifically directed by the manufacturer.

Browning Dish or Skillet

A browning dish is a special dish which, when preheated in the microwave oven, will become very hot over the base. Several shapes and sizes are available, either with a lid or without. The dish is used to brown such foods as chops, sausages, hamburgers, bacon, eggs etc. The food must be turned to brown on the other side. The deep

**Herby Roast Chicken (left),
Devilled Pork Chops (below)
and Chicken Breasts in Garlic
Cream Sauce (right).**

Variable Power Chart

MICROWAVE POWER LEVEL	DESCRIPTION AND SUGGESTED USE
10 or Full–High	Microwave energy constant at full wattage. For cooking vegetables, poultry, fish and some sauces, start joints.
8 or Roast	Power on for 13 seconds, auto cut-out for 2 seconds. Repeated continually for time selected, for reheating some joints.
7 and 6 – Medium	Power is on for about 10 seconds, off for 5 seconds, for chops, meat balls, chicken pieces, cakes.
4 and 5 – Simmer	Power is on for 6 seconds, off for 9 seconds, for completing casseroles, defrosting large joints, egg and cheese dishes.
3 – Defrost	Generally for defrosting (allow a standing time afterwards), for melting chocolate, and for delicate sauces.
2 – Very Low	Power is on for 3 seconds, off for 12 seconds. Keep cooked food warm for up to ½ hour. Soften butter and cream cheese from refrigerator.

Please note that this chart is given only as a guide. The variable power dial differs slightly from manufacturer to manufacturer.

Cooked food reheats remarkably quickly without drying out. A chart is provided to give some of the most common foods. Allow a few minutes standing time, after reheating, and before serving.

GENERAL RULES FOR REHEATING.
1. Cover food, allowing steam to escape, unless told specifically not to cover.
2. Stir foods such as casseroles, baked beans, stewed fruits, halfway through reheating.
3. Allow a short standing time – 3-5 minutes before removing covering and serving.
4. Reheat small items, such as sausage rolls or sausages, arranged in ring fashion on outside edge of plate. Reheat on Power 4, or Simmer.

Re-heating Chart

TYPE OF FOOD & WEIGHT	COVER	STIRRING	POWER LEVEL	TIME
1 Plated Meal	Cling Film	–	Full	3-4 minutes
1 Large Macaroni Cheese	Cling Film	Yes, once	Power 7 or Roast	10 minutes
2 Bowls Soup	–	Yes, once	Full	5 minutes
Baked Beans 100g (4ozs)	–	–	Power 7 or Roast	2 minutes
Baked Beans 450g (16ozs)	Yes	Yes, twice	Power 7 or Roast	7 minutes
Chicken Pieces 2 x 225g (8ozs)	Yes	–	Full	3-4 minutes
Beef Casserole for 4	Yes	Yes, twice	Full	10-12 minutes
Cooked Vegetables 100g (4ozs)	Yes	–	Full	45 seconds
Cooked Vegetables 450g (1lb)	Yes	Yes, once	Full	2 minutes
1 Family Meat Pie	No	No	4 or Simmer	7-8 minutes
6 Mince Pies	No	No	4 or Simmer	4 minutes
4 Bread Rolls	Kitchen Roll	No	4 or Simmer	2 minutes
Christmas Pudding 750g (1½lb)	Cling Film	No	Power 7 or Roast	3 minutes
Sauce 300ml (½ pt)	Cling Film	Yes, twice	Full	2 minutes
Fish 350g (12ozs)	Cling Film	–	Full	2 minutes

Defrosting Chart

FOOD TO BE DEFROSTED AND WEIGHT	POWER LEVEL	MICROWAVE TIME	STANDING TIME
Mince 450g (1lb)	4 or Defrost	6 minutes	15 minutes
Chicken 1½kg (3lb)	4 or Defrost	30 minutes	30 minutes
Joint of Beef 1½kg (3lb)	4 or Defrost	20 minutes	30 minutes
Shepherd's Pie 450g (1lb)	4 or Defrost	8 minutes	10 minutes
Large Lasagne	6 or Simmer	20 minutes	15 minutes
Chops 450g (1lb)	4 or Defrost	6 minutes	10 minutes
Sausages 450g (1lb)	4 or Defrost	6 minutes	10 minutes
Cod 225g (8ozs)	4 or Defrost	6 minutes	10 minutes
Raspberries 225g (8ozs)	4 or Defrost	4 minutes	15 minutes
1 Victoria Sandwich (2 egg)	4 or Defrost	2-3 minutes	15 minutes
Large Sliced Loaf	4 or Defrost	7 minutes	10 minutes
Cheese Sauce 300ml (½ Pint)	4 or Defrost	7 minutes	7 minutes
Chicken in Sauce for 4	Simmer	12 minutes	10 minutes
Family Apple Pie	4 or Defrost	8 minutes	5 minutes
Family Meat Pie or Quiche Lorraine	4 or Defrost	6-7 minutes	10 minutes

The microwave oven makes a perfect partner for your freezer as it enables you to defrost frozen foods in a fraction of the time that it would normally take. Remember to turn or stir the foods, for more even defrosting, and remember that a standing time is very important.

ALTERING TIMINGS

The recipes given in this book can be cooked in any model of variable power microwave oven that is available today. Each of these recipes was tested in a 700W microwave oven. Convert the timings in the following way, if the output of your oven is other than 700W:–

If using an oven of 500W, add 40 seconds for each minute stated in the recipe.

If using an oven of 600W, add 20 seconds for each minute stated in the recipe.

If using an oven of 650W plus, you will only need to allow a slight increase in the overall time.

browning dishes with lids are also used as casserole dishes. **These containers must not be used in conventional ovens.**

Stirring and Turning

Stirring and turning are methods used to equalise the heat in the food, i.e. the cooking of the food. The amount of stirring or turning will be governed by the type of food to be cooked, the cooking time and the even distribution of energy in the microwave oven. The recipes in this book give you a guide as to when to stir and turn. Adjust, if necessary, according to your own particular oven. Arrange foods such as baked apples or jacket potatoes in a ring fashion, leaving a space in the centre.

Starting Temperature of Food

The starting temperature of food will alter the cooking time. It may be at average room temperature, at cold room temperature or taken from the refrigerator or cold larder. Please note that the timings in this book are calculated for food at average room temperature, unless otherwise stated.

Can You Cook a Complete Meal by Microwave?

The easiest way to use a microwave oven is to employ stage cookery. The microwave oven cooks according to weight and time, not by temperature, and different types of food require different cooking times. During the standing time of the denser foods, such as joints and jacket potatoes, the less dense items, such as vegetables and sauces, are completely cooked. Foods of similar density may be cooked together, e.g. potatoes and carrots, but remember that the total energy available in the microwave oven must be shared between the foods introduced. If carrots and potatoes are cooked simultaneously, the resulting weight must be checked, and the cooking time calculated accordingly.

Some Things Cannot be Done

Do not try to cook Yorkshire puddings or other batter recipes, boil eggs, deep fat fry, or produce really crisp foods such as roast potatoes, as none of these will be successful. **Pastry** – baking blind, suet crust and some puff pastry recipes work beautifully, but do not try to cook the top of an apple pie. Baked pies may be reheated successfully on Simmer, or Power 4 – see chart.

Soups and Starters

Vegetable Soup

PREPARATION TIME:	10 minutes
MICROWAVE TIME:	21-26 minutes
SERVES:	4 people

25g (1oz) butter
450g (1lb) young leeks, cleaned and
    sliced
1 medium onion, peeled and sliced
175g (6oz) potato, peeled and diced
1 carrot, peeled and diced
Salt and freshly ground black pepper
    to taste
15ml (1 tblsp) chopped fresh parsley
450ml (¾ pint) homemade chicken
    stock
300ml (½ pint) milk

Melt the butter in a 2¼ litre (4 pint) casserole dish. Microwave on Full Power for 1 minute. Stir in all the prepared vegetables, salt and pepper, parsley and 45ml (3 tblsp) of the stock. Cover the dish, piercing the cling film if used. Microwave on Full Power for 12 minutes. Stir. Set aside, covered, for 5 minutes. Transfer the vegetables into the food processor bowl or liquidizer goblet; add the milk and liquidize or process until smooth. Return to the casserole and stir in the remaining stock. Microwave on Full Power, covered, for 3-5 minutes. Stir well before serving.

Asparagus with Mayonnaise

PREPARATION TIME:	10 minutes
MICROWAVE TIME:	10-12 minutes
SERVES:	4 people

450g (1lb) frozen asparagus spears
250ml (8 fl oz) corn oil
25g (1oz) butter
1 egg
1 egg yolk
150ml (¼ pint) olive oil
Salt and freshly ground black pepper
    to taste
30ml (2 tblsp) lemon juice
Chopped fresh parsley

Arrange the asparagus in a roasta bag in a suitable dish. Add 45ml (3 tblsp) water to the bag, with the butter. Seal the bag with a rubber

band. Pierce the bag once at the base. Microwave on Full Power for 10-12 minutes, turning the bag over once halfway through cooking time. Set aside. Put the egg and egg yolk into the goblet of a food processor or liquidizer with the salt and pepper. Blend on maximum. Add the oil, in a steady trickle, blending to a smooth mayonnaise. Add the lemon juice. Carefully drain the asparagus and arrange on a heated serving dish. Sprinkle with the parsley and serve accompanied by the mayonnaise. Serve immediately.

Soured Cream Prawns

PREPARATION TIME:	5 minutes
MICROWAVE TIME:	7-8 minutes
SERVES:	4 people

50g (2oz) butter
225g (8oz) peeled shrimps
Freshly ground black pepper to taste
1 egg yolk
150ml (¼ pint) soured cream
Paprika

Butter 4 ramekin dishes and divide the shrimps amongst them. Season well with black pepper. Combine the egg yolk and soured cream and spoon over the shrimps. Dot with the remaining butter. Microwave all 4 ramekins together on Power 4, or Simmer, for 7-8 minutes. (The dishes should be arranged in a ring, leaving a space in the centre.) Serve immediately sprinkled with paprika.

Sweetcorn Starter

PREPARATION TIME:	5 minutes
MICROWAVE TIME:	15 minutes
SERVES:	4 people

4 corn cobs
Sprigs of fresh savory
Salt and freshly ground black pepper
    to taste
100g (4oz) butter

Arrange the cobs in a suitable dish. Add 2-3 tblsp cold water and a few sprigs of savory. Season. Cover with cling film and pierce.

Microwave on Full Power for 6 minutes. Turn each cob over. Re-cover and microwave on Full Power for 6 minutes. Set aside. Put the butter into a 600ml (1 pint) jug and microwave on Power 4 or Simmer for about 3 minutes or until melted. Transfer the cooked cobs to a serving dish. Pour over the butter and sprinkle with extra chopped savory before serving.

Individual Frozen Pizzas

PREPARATION TIME:	2 minutes
MICROWAVE TIME:	6½-8½ minutes
SERVES:	1 person

Preheat a browning dish, without the lid, for 5-7 minutes. Put 15ml (1 tblsp) of oil and 1 individual pizza onto the dish. Microwave uncovered for approximately 1½ minutes on Full Power. Allow to stand for 1 minute before serving. As many pizzas as will fit onto your dish may be microwaved at the same time; increase the microwave time accordingly. Pizzas may be heated directly from the freezer, without the browning dish, on an ordinary non-metallic plate but the base will not be as crisp.

Chestnut Soup

PREPARATION TIME:	15 minutes
MICROWAVE TIME:	34 minutes
SERVES:	4 people

25g (1oz) butter
1 stem celery, chopped
2 large onions, chopped
900ml (1½ pint) homemade chicken
    stock (hot)
225g (8oz) unsweetened chestnut
    puree
Salt and freshly ground black pepper
    to taste
4 rashers streaky bacon, de-rinded

Put the butter, celery and onions into a 2¼ litre (4 pint) casserole dish; cover with a lid and microwave on Full Power for 4 minutes. Stir. Mix 300ml (½ pint) stock with the chestnut puree, in a 1.2 litre (2 pint) mixing bowl. Stir

into the onion mixture. Season with salt and black pepper; cover and microwave on Full Power for 7 minutes. Stir in the remaining stock and microwave on Full Power for 20 minutes. Allow to stand whilst preparing the bacon. Arrange the bacon on a microwave roasting rack, or on 2 sheets of absorbent kitchen paper. Microwave, uncovered, on Full Power, for about 3 minutes. Serve the soup sprinkled with the crumbled crispy bacon.

Tomato Baskets

PREPARATION TIME:	5 minutes
MICROWAVE TIME:	5½-6½ minutes
SERVES:	6 people

6 large firm tomatoes
225g (8oz) packet frozen mixed
    vegetables
50g (2oz) butter
Salt and freshly ground black pepper
    to taste
Few sprigs of fresh mint

Cut the top off each tomato and reserve. Using a grapefruit knife or a teaspoon, carefully scoop out the centre flesh. (Use in a soup or sauce recipe). Pierce the pouch of frozen vegetables once and place in a dish. Microwave on Full Power for 3½ minutes, turning the bag once halfway through the cooking time. Set aside. Stand the prepared tomatoes upright on a serving dish,

Asparagus with Mayonnaise (top), Vegetable Soup (centre) and Soured Cream Prawns (bottom).

in a ring. Dot with half the butter. Microwave on Full Power for about 2-3 minutes until very hot. Mix the drained, cooked vegetables with the remaining butter and salt and pepper and spoon into the tomato shells. Top with the reserved lids, and garnish with sprigs of mint. Serve immediately.

Quick Bap Pizzas

PREPARATION TIME: 10 minutes
MICROWAVE TIME: 6½-7½ minutes
SERVES: 4 as a main meal, 8 as a snack

4 baps
1 medium onion, finely chopped
5ml (1 tsp) tomato puree
5ml (1 tsp) dried oregano
225g (8oz) can tomatoes, chopped
5ml (1 tsp) French mustard
Salt and freshly ground black pepper to taste
150g (5oz) Cheddar cheese, thinly sliced or grated
Stuffed olives, sliced

Tomato Baskets (right), Quick Bap Pizzas (below) and Individual Frozen Pizza (far right).

Cut the baps in half and arrange in a ring on a suitable baking sheet. Place the onion in a 1.2 litre (2 pint) mixing bowl; cover and microwave for 1½ minutes on Full Power. Stir in the tomato puree, oregano, chopped tomatoes and the mustard. Season with salt and pepper. Divide amongst the baps, and cover with the cheese. Decorate with the sliced olives. Microwave on Power 4 for 5-6 minutes, until the cheese has melted. Serve immediately.

Garlic Prawn Starter

PREPARATION TIME: 30 minutes

MICROWAVE TIME: 20 minutes

SERVES: 4 people

750g (1½lb) courgettes, cleaned, topped and tailed
Salt and freshly ground black pepper to taste
350g (12oz) peeled prawns
15ml (1 tblsp) chopped chives
30ml (2 tblsp) dry white wine

2 cloves garlic, crushed
15ml (1 tblsp) lemon juice
50g (2oz) butter

Garnish
Unpeeled prawns

Slice the courgettes thinly into a colander, sprinkling them generously with salt. Cover with a plate and weigh down; leave to stand for 20 minutes. Rinse well under cold running water. Drain thoroughly. Arrange the courgettes

in a vegetable dish. Season with salt and pepper. Cover and microwave on Full Power for 12 minutes. Stir. Set aside, covered. Put the peeled prawns, chives, wine, garlic, lemon juice and butter into a 1.2 litre (2 pint) casserole. Cover with a lid. Microwave on Power 4, or Simmer, for 8 minutes. Stir once halfway through cooking time. Drain the excess liquid from the courgettes. Top with the heated prawns and their juices. Garnish with the unpeeled prawns and serve immediately.

Egg and Tuna Starter

PREPARATION TIME: 10 minutes

MICROWAVE TIME: 10 minutes

SERVES: 4 people

200g (7oz) can tuna fish in oil, drained
2 hard boiled eggs, cooked conventionally and chopped
300ml (½ pint) milk
25g (1oz) butter
Salt and freshly ground black pepper to taste
25g (1oz) plain flour
5ml (1 tsp) made mustard
50g (2oz) grated Cheddar cheese

Garnish
Stuffed olives, sliced

Flake the tuna fish and divide between 4 ramekin dishes. Top with the egg. Melt the butter in a 1 litre (1¾ pint) jug for 1 minute on Full Power, or until very hot. Stir in the flour and gradually stir in the milk. Microwave on Full Power for 2 minutes. Beat well with a balloon whisk. Microwave on Full Power for 2 minutes. Beat well with a balloon whisk. Beat in salt and pepper and cheese. Divide the sauce amongst the ramekins. Garnish with sliced olives. Microwave all 4 ramekins together for 5 minutes on Power 4 or Simmer. Serve immediately.

Mackerel Pate

PREPARATION TIME: 10 minutes plus chilling

MICROWAVE TIME: 3 minutes

SERVES: 6 people

1 onion, finely chopped
50g (2oz) butter
225g (8oz) cream cheese
30ml (2 tblsp) lemon juice
30ml (2 tblsp) chopped fresh parsley

350g (12oz) smoked mackerel fillets
5ml (1 tsp) coarse French mustard
Freshly ground black pepper to taste
45ml (3 tblsp) soured cream
10ml (2 tsp) tomato puree

Garnish
Lemon wedges
Fresh parsley and cucumber slices

Put the onion into a soup bowl. Cover with cling film and pierce. Microwave on Full Power for 1 minute. Set aside. Flake the fish into the food processor or liquidizer goblet, discarding skin and bones. Add the onion. Place the butter in the bowl used for the onion and microwave on Power 4, or Simmer, for 2 minutes. Add to the processor or liquidizer with all the remaining ingredients. Process or liquidize until smooth. Pour into a dampened loaf tin; smooth the surface. Chill until firm. Turn out onto a serving dish and garnish with wedges of lemon, crimped cucumber slices and parsley.

This page: Sweetcorn Starter (top), Garlic Prawn Starter (bottom).

All types of vegetables, both frozen and fresh, microwave exceptionally well. They keep their colour, flavour and shape. Follow a few simple rules and use the charts to help you.

Helpful Hints
1. If you want to add salt, dissolve it in a little water beforehand. Adding salt can cause some vegetables to dry; to be on the safe side season with salt after cooking.
2. Always cover vegetables – roasta or freezer bags are very useful, but remember to pierce them.
3. Stir at least once during the cooking time or, if using a bag, turn it over.
4. Add only the amount of water necessary.
5. Cut the vegetables into even sized pieces.
6. Allow a standing time after cooking and before serving.
7. Cook frozen vegetables from frozen, do not defrost them first.

Baked Stuffed Marrow

| PREPARATION TIME: 20 minutes |
| MICROWAVE TIME: 22 minutes |
| SERVES: 4 people |

1 medium size marrow
25g (1oz) butter
1 onion, peeled and finely chopped
450g (1lb) raw, lean minced beef
15g (½oz) plain flour
5ml (1 tsp) dried basil or oregano
1 egg, beaten
1 beef stock cube, crumbled
Salt and freshly ground black pepper to taste
15ml (1 tblsp) tomato puree

Wipe the marrow with a damp cloth. Cut both ends off the marrow and keep on one side. Scoop out the seeds with a spoon and discard. Melt the butter in a 1.75 litre (3 pint) mixing bowl for 1 minute on Full Power. Stir in the onion. Microwave on Full Power for 1 minute. Stir in all the remaining ingredients. Mix well. Secure one end of the marrow with wooden cocktail sticks. Stuff the marrow with the mince mixture. Secure the remaining end in place

Fresh Vegetable Chart

VEGETABLE AND WEIGHT	ADDITION	MICROWAVE TIME	STANDING TIME
Sliced Green Beans 450g (1lb)	45ml (3 tblsp) water	8 minutes	5 minutes
Broad Beans 450g (1lb)	45ml (3 tblsp) water	8 minutes	5 minutes
Broccoli Spears 225g (8ozs)	45ml (3 tblsp) water	7 minutes	4 minutes
Sliced Carrots 450g (1lb)	30ml (2 tblsp) water	7-8 minutes	4 minutes
Cauliflower Florets 450g (1lb)	45ml (3 tblsp) water	7-8 minutes	5 minutes
Chopped Celery 225g (8ozs)	45ml (3 tblsp) water	7 minutes	4 minutes
Courgettes 450g (1lb)	25g (1oz) butter	10 minutes	3 minutes
Leeks 450g (1lb)	30ml (2 tblsp) water	7-8 minutes	3 minutes
Mushrooms (Sliced) 225g (8ozs)	25g (1oz) butter	2 minutes	2 minutes
Sliced Marrow 450g (1lb)	25g (1oz) butter	7 minutes	3 minutes
New Potatoes 450g (1lb)	30ml (2 tblsp) water	7 minutes	4 minutes
Old Potatoes 450g (1lb)	45ml (3 tblsp) water	9 minutes	5 minutes
Sliced Onions 450g (1lb)	30ml (2 tblsp) water	8-9 minutes	4 minutes
Brussels Sprouts 450g (1lb)	30ml (2 tblsp) water	6-7 minutes	4 minutes
Diced Swede 450g (1lb)	30ml (2 tblsp) water	13 minutes	6 minutes

with wooden cocktail sticks. Place the marrow on a meat roasting rack and cover with cling film. Pierce. Microwave on Full Power for about 20 minutes, turning the marrow once halfway through cooking time. Allow to stand, covered with foil, for 5 minutes before serving. Cut into rings, and serve piping hot.

Brussels Sprouts with Chestnut and Bacon

| PREPARATION TIME: 15 minutes |
| MICROWAVE TIME: 8 minutes |
| SERVES: 4 people |

450g (1lb) fresh Brussels sprouts
15ml (1 tblsp) lemon juice
5ml (1 tsp) dried mixed herbs
30ml (2 tblsp) cold water
Salt and freshly ground black pepper to taste
75g (3oz) butter
225g (8oz) canned whole chestnuts, drained
3 rashers streaky bacon, de-rinded, cooked and chopped (see Garlic Mushrooms recipe)

Peel the sprouts and make a cross in the base of each one. Put the sprouts into a 1.2 litre (2 pint) casserole dish, or into a roasta bag. Add the lemon juice, herbs, water, and salt and pepper. Cover with a lid, or pierce the bag if used. Microwave on Full Power for 5 minutes. Stir or turn once, halfway through cooking time. Set aside for 5 minutes. Put the butter into a 300ml (½ pint) Pyrex jug and microwave on Power 4 or Simmer until melted (about 3 minutes). If

using a roasta bag, tip the sprouts into serving dish. Add the chestnuts to the Brussels sprouts, stirring gently. Cover with a lid. Microwave on Full Power for 1 minute. Coat with melted butter, sprinkle with chopped bacon, and serve.

Brussels Sprouts with Chestnut and Bacon (top), Carrot and Parsnip Puree (centre) and Baked Stuffed Marrow (bottom).

Frozen Vegetable Chart

VEGETABLE AND WEIGHT	AMOUNT OF WATER	COOKING TIME	STANDING TIME
Asparagus 225g (8ozs)	30ml (2 tblsp)	7 minutes	5 minutes
Broccoli 225g (8ozs)	45ml (3 tblsp)	10 minutes	5 minutes
Brussels Sprouts 225g (8ozs)	30ml (2 tblsp)	4 minutes	3 minutes
Carrots 225g (8ozs)	30ml (2 tblsp)	6 minutes	3 minutes
Cauliflower Florets 225g (8ozs)	30ml (2 tblsp)	3 minutes	2 minutes
Courgettes 225g (8ozs)	Nil	4 minutes	2 minutes
Leeks 225g (8ozs)	30ml (2 tblsp)	6-7 minutes	2 minutes
Mixed Vegetables 225g (8ozs)	30ml (2 tblsp)	4 minutes	3 minutes
Mushrooms 225g (8ozs)	25g (1oz) butter and herbs	4 minutes	2 minutes
Baby Onions 225g (8ozs)	25g (1oz) butter	5 minutes	4 minutes
Peas 225g (8ozs)	Nil	4 minutes	2 minutes
Spinach 225g (8ozs)	Nil	5 minutes	3 minutes
Sweetcorn 225g (8ozs)	Nil	4 minutes	2 minutes

Carrot and Parsnip Puree

PREPARATION TIME: 15 minutes

MICROWAVE TIME: 13 minutes

SERVES: 4 people

225g (8oz) carrots, peeled
225g (8oz) parsnips, peeled
2.5ml (½ tsp) dried basil
45ml (3 tblsp) well-flavoured stock
30ml (2 tblsp) double cream
Salt and freshly ground black pepper to taste
Pinch grated nutmeg

Garnish
Carrot curls

Dice the peeled carrots and parsnips and place in a roasta bag in a 1.2 litre (2 pint) casserole. Add 30ml (2 tblsp) water and the basil. Snip the bag once at the base. Microwave on Full Power for 8 minutes, turning the bag over once halfway through cooking time. Set aside for 5 minutes. Empty the contents of the roasta bag into the goblet of a food processor or liquidizer. Add the stock and process until smooth. Add cream, salt and pepper, and nutmeg.

Process just to blend. Return to the casserole and cover with a lid. Microwave on Power 4, or Simmer, for 5 minutes. Garnish with carrot curls and serve.

Courgette Choice

PREPARATION TIME: 40-45 minutes

COOKING TIME: 10 minutes

SERVES: 4 people

450g (1lb) young courgettes, topped, tailed and washed
Salt and freshly ground black pepper to taste
450g (1lb) large firm tomatoes, skinned and sliced
2.5ml (½ tsp) dried tarragon
1 clove garlic, crushed
25g (1oz) butter

Arrange the sliced courgettes in a colander. Sprinkle generously with salt and leave to stand for 30 minutes. (This draws out the bitter juices.) Rinse well under cold running water. Drain. Layer the courgettes and tomatoes in a 1.2 litre (2 pint) casserole dish, starting and finishing with courgettes.

Season each layer with salt, pepper, tarragon and garlic. Dot the top with small knobs of butter. Cover tightly with a lid. Microwave on Full Power for 10 minutes. Allow to stand for 3 minutes before serving.

Cauliflower Cheese

PREPARATION TIME: 10 minutes

MICROWAVE TIME: 12 minutes

SERVES: 4 people

1 cauliflower, trimmed and divided into florets
15g (½oz) cornflour
300ml (½ pint) milk
5ml (1 tsp) made mustard
Salt and freshly ground black pepper to taste
75g (3oz) grated Cheddar cheese
25g (1oz) butter
½ red pepper, de-seeded and chopped

Arrange the florets of cauliflower in a roasta bag. Add 30ml (2 tblsp) water. Pierce the bag, and place in a 1.2 litre (2 pint) casserole. Microwave on Full Power for 7-8 minutes, turning the bag over once

halfway through cooking time. Set aside, covered. Cream the cornflour with a little of the milk to a smooth paste. Stir in the mustard and salt and pepper to taste. Heat the remaining milk in a 1 litre (1¾ pint) jug for 2 minutes on Full Power. Pour the heated milk onto the cornflour mixture, stirring continuously. Return to the jug and microwave on Full Power for 2 minutes or until boiling. Beat in the cheese and butter, and any liquid from the cauliflower. Transfer cauliflower florets to a warmed serving dish. Pour the sauce over evenly. Sprinkle with the red pepper and serve immediately. The red pepper may be heated in a cup in the microwave for 1 minute on Full Power, if liked.

Ratatouille

PREPARATION TIME: 40 minutes

MICROWAVE TIME: 22-24 minutes

SERVES: 4 people

225g (½lb) courgettes
450g (1lb) aubergines
Salt and freshly ground black pepper to taste
50g (2oz) butter
1 medium onion, peeled and sliced
1 large clove garlic, crushed
A little oil
1 red pepper, de-seeded and sliced
425g (15oz) can tomatoes, chopped
2.5ml (½ tsp) dried oregano
50g (2oz) crumbled Danish Blue cheese

Wash the courgettes and aubergines. Cut off the ends and discard. Slice into ½ cm (¼ inch) slices and layer with a generous sprinkling of salt in a colander. Top with a plate and a weight and set aside to drain for 15 minutes. Rinse well under cold running water and drain. Put the butter in a 600ml (1 pint) measuring jug. Microwave on Full Power for 1-2 minutes until melted. Stir in the onion and garlic. Grease the sides and base of a 1.75-2.25 litre (3-4 pint) casserole or souffle dish with

Ratatouille (top), Courgette Choice (centre left) and Cauliflower Cheese (bottom).

oil. Layer the aubergines, courgettes and red pepper in the dish with the tomatoes, oregano, onion and garlic. Season each layer with salt and pepper. Cover with a lid. Microwave on Full Power for 20-22 minutes, removing the lid for the last 8 minutes. Turn the dish ¼ turn twice during the cooking time, if necessary. Top with the crumbled cheese and serve immediately.

Buttery Mashed Potato

PREPARATION TIME: 10 minutes
MICROWAVE TIME: 17 minutes
SERVES: 4-5 people

1kg (2lb) old potatoes, peeled
45ml (3 tblsp) milk
50g (2oz) butter
Salt and freshly ground black pepper to taste
50ml (2 tblsp) single cream
Chopped fresh parsley

Cut the potatoes into small, even sized pieces and put into a roasta bag with the milk and butter. Season. Secure the bag with an elastic band and stand in a 1.75 litre (3 pint) mixing bowl. Pierce the bag once at the base. Microwave on Full Power for 17 minutes, turning the bag over once halfway through the cooking time. Allow to stand for 5 minutes. Turn the potatoes and their liquid into the bowl and mash with a fork. Beat with a wooden spoon adding the cream. Turn into a serving dish. Fork up and sprinkle with the parsley. Serve.

Potatoes Gratinee

PREPARATION TIME: 20 minutes
MICROWAVE TIME: 26 minutes
SERVES: 4 people

750g (1½lb) old white potatoes, peeled and thinly sliced
300ml (½ pint) pouring white sauce
50g (2oz) grated cheese
45ml (3 tblsp) milk
Salt and freshly ground black pepper to taste
25g (1oz) butter
1 Recipe quantity of Crispy Topping (see recipe)

Soak the potato slices in cold water for a few minutes. Heat the sauce in a large jug for 1 minute on Full Power. Beat in the grated cheese, milk, and salt and pepper to taste. Grease a shallow dish with the butter. Arrange the drained potato slices, overlapping slightly, in the

Spinach Fiesta (top), Buttery Mashed Potato (far left) and Potatoes Gratinee (left).

base of the dish. Pour the sauce evenly over the top. Cover with cling film and pierce. Microwave on Power 7, or Roast, for 25 minutes. Stir once, gently, halfway through cooking time. Serve after 5 minutes standing time, sprinkled with the crispy topping.

Stuffed Baked Peppers

PREPARATION TIME: 10 minutes

MICROWAVE TIME: 14½-15½ minutes

SERVES: 4 people

4 large, even-sized peppers, about 225g (8oz) each
30ml (2 tblsp) water
350g (12oz) cooked chicken, pork or turkey
30ml (2 tblsp) drained, canned sweetcorn kernels
60ml (4 tblsp) soured cream
75g (3oz) chopped button mushrooms
Salt and freshly ground black pepper to taste

Cut the tops off the peppers and reserve. Scoop out the seeds and discard them. Stand the peppers upright in an oblong or round casserole dish. Add the water; cover and microwave on Full Power for 3½ minutes. Set aside. Combine all the remaining ingredients to make the filling and mix well. Drain the water from the peppers and divide the filling amongst them. Replace the tops. Cover with cling film and pierce. Microwave on Full Power for 11-12 minutes. Stand for 3 minutes before serving.

Garlic Mushrooms

PREPARATION TIME: 20 minutes

MICROWAVE TIME: 12½-14½

SERVES: 4 people

75g (3oz) butter
2 cloves garlic, crushed
350g (12oz) button mushrooms, stalks removed
4 rashers streaky bacon, de-rinded
100g (4oz) cream cheese
Salt and freshly ground black pepper to taste
15ml (1 tblsp) natural yogurt or soured cream
2.5ml (½ tsp) dried parsley

Garnish
Chopped fresh parsley

Place the butter and garlic into a small bowl and microwave on Power 4, or Simmer, for 3 minutes, or until melted. Using a pastry brush, brush the mushrooms all over, inside and out, with the melted butter. Arrange on a dinner plate, or baking sheet, in a circular fashion, leaving a space in the centre. Arrange the bacon on 2 sheets of absorbent kitchen paper, on a dinner plate, fat to outside. Cover with 1 piece absorbent kitchen paper. Microwave the bacon on Full Power for 2½-3 minutes. Set aside. Transfer the cream cheese to a 1.2 litre (2 pint) mixing bowl. Microwave, uncovered, on Defrost for 2 minutes. Stir in salt and pepper to taste, yogurt, dried parsley and chopped bacon. Soften the chopped onion in a cup for 45 seconds on Full Power. Stir into the cream cheese mixture. Fill the mushrooms with the cheese mixture. Microwave, uncovered on Roast, or Power 7, for 4-6 minutes. Serve immediately garnished with chopped parsley, on croutons of fried bread.

Spinach Fiesta

PREPARATION TIME: 20 minutes

MICROWAVE TIME: 22 minutes

SERVES: 4 people

225g (8oz) long grain rice
Salt and freshly ground black pepper to taste
3 frozen cod steaks
225g (8oz) frozen spinach
25g (1oz) butter
50ml (2 tblsp) milk
30ml (2 tblsp) canned tuna fish, drained
50g (2oz) Cheddar cheese, cubed
Chopped fresh parsley

Put the rice into a 1.75-2.25 litre (3-4 pint) mixing bowl. Pour on 600ml (1 pint) boiling water. Add 2.5ml (½ tsp) salt. Cover lightly with cling film and pierce once in the centre. Microwave on Full Power for 12 minutes. Set aside. Snip the fish packets open and microwave all 3 together, arranged on a dinner plate in a ring, for 6 minutes on Defrost. Turn each packet over, halfway through cooking. Set aside. Pierce the packet of spinach and place in a vegetable dish. Microwave on Full Power for 6 minutes. Set aside. Slip the cod steaks out of their packets and arrange on a pie plate in a ring.

Dot with butter. Season and spoon over the milk. Cover with cling film and pierce. Microwave on Full Power for 4 minutes. Drain the spinach. Chop and fork into the cooked rice. Add the tuna fish to the rice with the cheese. Drain the cooked cod and flake into the rice. Pile onto a warmed dish and serve, sprinkled with plenty of chopped parsley.

JACKET POTATOES WITH FILLINGS

Plain Jacket Potatoes

PREPARATION TIME: 15-20 minutes

MICROWAVE TIME: 15 minutes

SERVES: 4 people

4 x 200g (7oz) potatoes, scrubbed clean

Prick the potatoes with a fork and arrange in a ring on a dinner plate. Microwave uncovered, on Full Power, for 15 minutes. Wrap in a clean tea towel and set aside for 10-15 minutes. (The potatoes will continue to cook). Meanwhile prepare one of the fillings (all fillings serve 4 people).

Cottage Cheese with Prawns and Chives

Instead of pricking the potatoes, make a cross in the top of each one before baking.

225g (8oz) cottage cheese
15ml (1 tblsp) chopped chives
100g (4oz) peeled prawns
15ml (1 tblsp) soured cream
5ml (1 tsp) tomato puree
Sliced cucumber and whole prawns to garnish

Blend all the ingredients together, apart from the cucumber and prawns. Using a cloth, carefully push up each hot potato from the base, to form a water lily. Divide the filling between the potatoes. Garnish with the cucumber and whole prawns before serving.

Pilchards with Corn

30ml (2 tblsp) natural yogurt or mayonnaise
Salt and freshly ground black pepper to taste

350g (12oz) pilchards in tomato sauce
45ml (3 tblsp) drained canned sweetcorn kernels
4 spring onions, chopped

Cut the potatoes in half and carefully scoop out the flesh, leaving the skin intact. Put the potato flesh into a 1.75 litre (3 pint) mixing bowl. Mash well with a fork, adding the yogurt or mayonnaise and salt and pepper to taste. Open each pilchard and remove the backbone. Flake the pilchards into the potato; mix well, adding the sweetcorn and chopped spring onion. Pile the mixture back into the potato shells. Arrange in a serving dish. Cover with cling film. Microwave on Full Power for 4 minutes.

Baked Beans with Edam Cheese

425g (15.9oz) can baked beans in tomato sauce
225g (8oz) Edam cheese, cubed
Salt and freshly ground black pepper to taste

Garnish
Watercress

Empty the beans into a 900ml (1½pint) casserole dish. Add the cheese and salt and pepper to taste. Cover with a lid and microwave on Power 7, or Roast, for 2½ minutes. Stir gently. Microwave on Power 7, or Roast, for 2½ minutes. Halve the potatoes after their standing time. Spoon the beans and cheese onto the potatoes. Garnish with watercress and serve.

Stuffed Baked Peppers (top), Jacket Potatoes with Fillings (centre) and Garlic Mushrooms (bottom).

Supper Dishes

Shish Kebabs

PREPARATION TIME: 10 minutes
MICROWAVE TIME: 8 minutes
SERVES: 3-4 people

350g (12oz) raw minced lamb
1 onion, finely chopped
10ml (2 tsp) lemon juice
5-10ml (1-2 tsp) mild curry powder
15ml (1 tblsp) soured cream
½ egg, beaten
25g (1oz) plain flour
30ml (2 tblsp) finely chopped fresh
 parsley
2.5ml (½ tsp) salt
15ml (1 tblsp) tomato sauce

Mix all the ingredients together.
Form the mixture into small balls.
Arrange the meatballs on a
microwave roasting rack in a ring.
Microwave, uncovered, on Power
7, or Roast, for 8 minutes. Serve
hot with yogurt sauce.

Yogurt Sauce

PREPARATION TIME: 5 minutes
SERVES: 4 people

150ml (5 fl oz) natural yogurt
5ml (1 tsp) granular mustard
10ml (2 tsp) tomato puree
5ml (1 tsp) concentrated mint sauce
5ml (1 tsp) lemon juice
5ml (1 tsp) caster sugar
30ml (2 tblsp) soured cream

Mix all the ingredients together
until well blended. Refrigerate until
required. Serve with Shish Kebabs.

Pasta Shells with Cheese and Bacon

PREPARATION TIME: 15 minutes
MICROWAVE TIME: 24 minutes
SERVES: 4 people

175g (6oz) dried pasta shapes
2.5ml (½ tsp) salt
15ml (1 tblsp) oil
225g (8oz) packet frozen mixed
 vegetables
5ml (1 tsp) cornflour
300ml (½ pint) milk

5ml (1 tsp) made mustard
Salt and freshly ground black pepper
 to taste
75g (3oz) grated Red Leicester cheese
2 bacon chops
1 Recipe Crispy Topping (see recipe)

Place the pasta in a 2.25-2.75 litre
(4-5 pint) mixing bowl. Add the
salt and the oil. Pour on 1.75 litres
(3 pints) boiling water. Cover
tightly with cling film and pierce
once in the centre. Microwave on
Full Power for 8 minutes. Set aside,
covered. Microwave the pierced
packet of vegetables in a suitable
dish, for 4 minutes on Full Power,
turning the packet over once
halfway through the cooking time.
Blend the cornflour with 15ml (1
tblsp) milk until smooth. Put the
remaining milk into a 1 litre (1¾
pint) jug and microwave on Full
Power for 3 minutes. Beat the
blended cornflour into the hot
milk together with the mustard and
salt and pepper to taste.
Microwave on Full Power for 2
minutes. Beat well adding the
cheese Microwave the bacon chops
on 2 sheets of absorbent kitchen
paper (with the fat facing
outwards). Microwave on Roast for
4 minutes. To assemble the dish:
drain the pasta and pile onto a
serving dish; drain the vegetables
and add to the pasta; chop the
bacon and mix into the pasta and
vegetables. Pour the cheese sauce
evenly over the top and top with
crispy crumbs. Microwave on
Power 5, or Roast, for 3 minutes.
Serve immediately.

Fish Fingers

PREPARATION TIME: 5 minutes
MICROWAVE TIME: 14 minutes
SERVES: 3-4 people

30ml (2 tblsp) cooking oil
8 frozen cod fish fingers

Preheat a large browning dish,
without a lid, for 7 minutes, on Full
Power. Put the oil into the heated
dish. Microwave on Full Power for
1 minute. Carefully press the fish
fingers into the oil. Microwave,
uncovered, on Full Power for 3

minutes. Turn each fish finger over
and microwave on Full Power for 3-
4 minutes. Drain on absorbent
kitchen paper and serve immediately (brown side uppermost).

Crispy Topping

PREPARATION TIME: 10 minutes
MICROWAVE TIME: 8 minutes

65g (2½oz) butter
100g (4oz) fresh brown breadcrumbs
50g (2oz) oatmeal

Put the butter into a 1.75 litre (3
pint) mixing bowl and microwave
on Full Power for 1½ minutes. Stir
in the breadcrumbs and oatmeal.
Microwave on Full Power for 2½
minutes. Stir with a fork.
Microwave on Full Power for 2
minutes. Stir. Microwave on Full
Power for 2 minutes. Allow to
stand for 5 minutes before using.
Alternatively, the topping may be
cooled and stored in an airtight
container. Serve as a crispy finish
for sweet and savoury dishes.

Kidney and Sausage Supper Dish

PREPARATION TIME: 20 minutes
MICROWAVE TIME: 18 minutes
SERVES: 4 people

450g (1lb) chipolata sausages
30ml (2 tblsp) oil
225g (8oz) lambs' kidneys, skinned,
 halved and cored
30ml (2 tblsp) tomato sauce
15ml (1 tblsp) Worcestershire sauce
Salt and freshly ground black pepper
 to taste
4 large, ripe tomatoes, skinned and
 chopped
225g (8oz) frozen peas
10ml (2 tsp) cornflour

Preheat the deep browning dish,
without the lid, for 4-7 minutes
according to size. Prick the sausages
and cut into 2.5cm (1 inch) pieces.
Add the oil and the pieces of
sausage to the preheated dish,
pressing the sausage against the
sides of the browning dish.

Microwave on Full Power for 2
minutes. Stir in the kidneys,
tomato sauce and Worcestershire
sauce. Cover with the lid and
microwave on Power 7, or on
Roast, for 5 minutes. Season with
salt and pepper and stir in the
tomatoes and peas. Mix the
cornflour to a smooth paste with
60ml (4 tblsp) water and stir in.
Microwave on Full Power for 2
minutes. Stir. Microwave on Full
Power for a further 2 minutes. Stir
and serve immediately.

Cowboy Supper

PREPARATION TIME: 15 minutes
MICROWAVE TIME: 13 minutes
SERVES: 4 people

425g (15.9oz) can baked beans
200g (7oz) can corned beef, chilled
Freshly ground black pepper to taste
½ beef stock cube, crumbled
50g (2oz) Cheddar cheese, cubed
1 French loaf

Empty the baked beans into a 1.75
litre (3 pint) casserole dish. Cover
with a lid. Microwave on Power 6
for 5 minutes. Gently stir in the
corned beef and season with
pepper. Add the stock cube. Cover
and microwave on Power 6 for 5
minutes. Add the cheese just
before serving.
To warm the bread, cut the bread
into pieces and arrange in a bread
basket, between absorbent paper
napkins. Microwave on Power 4, or
Simmer, for 3 minutes. Serve
immediately.

**Shish Kebabs with Yogurt
Sauce (top), Pasta Shells with
Cheese and Bacon (centre
right) and Kidney and Sausage
Supper Dish (bottom).**

Poached Eggs on Cheese on Toast

PREPARATION TIME: 10 minutes

MICROWAVE TIME: about 10 minutes

SERVES: 4 people

4 eggs
Salt and freshly ground black pepper to taste
Softened butter
4 slices toast
150g (5oz) grated cheese
Chopped chives

Put 15ml (1 tblsp) cold water into each of the 4 hollows of a microwave muffin pan or into 4 ramekin dishes. If using ramekins, arrange them in a ring on a dinner plate. Microwave on Full Power until the water boils. Carefully crack 1 egg into each hollow or dish. Prick each yolk once with a cocktail stick. Season with salt and pepper. Microwave on Simmer for about 4 minutes until the whites are just set. Leave aside. Butter the toast and top with the grated cheese. Microwave on Power 5, or Simmer, for about 4 minutes until melted. Slide the toasted cheese onto a serving dish and place an egg on top of each one. Sprinkle with chopped chives and serve immediately.

Cod and Prawn Supper Dish

PREPARATION TIME: 15 minutes

MICROWAVE TIME: 15½ minutes

SERVES: 4 people

4 x 75g (3oz) frozen cod steaks, thawed
50g (2oz) butter
Salt and freshly ground black pepper to taste
25g (1oz) flour
300ml (½ pint) milk
75g (3oz) grated Cheddar cheese
100g (4oz) peeled prawns
1 Recipe Crispy Topping (see recipe)

Garnish
Tomato wedges
Parsley

Arrange the fish steaks in a ring on a dinner plate. Divide half the butter into 4; put a small knob onto each fish steak. Season with salt and pepper and cover with cling film. Microwave on Full Power for 3½ minutes. Set aside. Microwave the remaining butter in a 1 litre (1¾ pint) jug for 1 minute on Full Power. Stir in the flour and then gradually stir in the milk; season to taste. Microwave on Full Power for 2 minutes. Beat well. Microwave on Full Power for a further 2 minutes. Beat in the cheese. Cut the fish into bite-size pieces and arrange in a suitable dish with the prawns. Pour the sauce evenly over the fish. Sprinkle with the crispy crumbs. Microwave on Power 4 for 7 minutes. Serve immediately, garnished with tomato and parsley.

Chicken with Ham

PREPARATION TIME: 15 minutes

MICROWAVE TIME: 13 minutes

SERVES: 4 people

350g (12oz) cooked chicken, roughly chopped
100g (4oz) cooked ham, chopped
60ml (4 tblsp) drained canned sweetcorn kernels with peppers
25g (1oz) butter
25g (1oz) flour
Salt and freshly ground black pepper to taste
300ml (½ pint) well flavoured chicken stock
75g (3oz) grated cheese
45ml (3 tblsp) single cream

Garnish
Sliced tomato and parsley

Arrange the chicken, ham and sweetcorn in a suitable dish. Melt the butter in a large jug for about 1 minute on Full Power. Stir in the flour and salt and pepper to taste. Stir in a little of the stock, blending it in well. Add the remaining stock. Microwave on Full Power for 2 minutes. Beat well with a balloon whisk. Microwave on Full Power for 2 minutes. Beat well. Beat in the cheese and the cream. Pour the sauce evenly over the meat. Microwave on Power 4, or Simmer, for about 8 minutes. Serve immediately, garnished with the tomato and parsley.

Sweet and Sour Pork

PREPARATION TIME: 25 minutes

MICROWAVE TIME: 29 minutes

SERVES: 4 people

15ml (1 tblsp) oil
½ red pepper, de-seeded and chopped
1 carrot, peeled and cut into strips
1 large onion, sliced
10cm (4 inch) cucumber, seeded and cut into strips
1 stem celery, chopped
450g (1lb) pork fillet, cubed
400g (14oz) can pineapple pieces in natural juice

**Fish Fingers (top right),
Poached Eggs on Cheese on
Toast (far left) and Chicken
with Ham (left).**

30ml (2 tblsp) soya sauce
10ml (2 tsp) tomato puree
15ml (1 tblsp) wine vinegar
Salt and freshly ground black pepper
   to taste
10ml (2 tsp) cornflour

Preheat the deep browning dish

without the lid for 4-7 minutes
according to size on Full Power. Put
the oil, pepper, carrot, onion,
cucumber and celery into the dish.
Stir well. Cover and Microwave on
Full Power for 4 minutes. Stir in all
remaining ingredients, apart from
the cornflour. Cover and

microwave on Full Power for 3
minutes and then on Power 4, or
Simmer, for 20 minutes. Cream the
cornflour with a little water and stir
into the pork mixture. Microwave
on Full Power for 2 minutes. Stir
and then serve immediately on a
bed of rice.

**Cowboy Supper (top) and
Sweet and Sour Pork (bottom).**

Fish Dishes

Plaice with Lemon

PREPARATION TIME: 12-15 minutes

MICROWAVE TIME: 9 minutes

SERVES: 4 people

4 plaice fillets (about 90g (3½oz) each), skinned
Salt and freshly ground black pepper to taste
Juice of ½ a lemon
30ml (2 tblsp) milk
100g (4oz) button mushrooms, sliced
25g (1oz) butter
120ml (4 fl oz) soured cream

Lay the plaice fillets out flat; season with salt and pepper and sprinkle with lemon juice. Roll up and secure with wooden cocktail sticks. Arrange the fillets close together in a dish and spoon over the milk; cover and microwave on Full Power for 5 minutes. Set aside. Put the mushrooms and butter into a small dish. Cover and microwave on Full Power for 2 minutes. Add the soured cream and stir in the juices from the fish. Microwave on Full Power for 2 minutes. Arrange the fish on a warmed serving dish. Pour over the sauce and serve immediately.

Curried Prawns with Chicken

PREPARATION TIME: 15 minutes

MICROWAVE TIME: about 22 minutes

SERVES: 4 people

50g (2oz) butter
1 medium onion, finely chopped
20ml (4 tsp) flour
20ml (4 tsp) mild curry powder
10ml (2 tsp) tomato puree
900ml (1½ pints) boiling chicken stock
15ml (1 tblsp) apple chutney
1 banana, thinly sliced
25g (1oz) raisins
Salt and freshly ground black pepper to taste
225g (8oz) peeled prawns
225g (8oz) cooked chicken, chopped
30ml (2 tblsp) lemon juice

Place the butter in a 2.25 litre (4 pint) casserole. Microwave on Full Power for 1-2 minutes. Stir in the onion. Microwave on Full Power for 1½ minutes. Stir in the flour and curry powder. Microwave on Full Power for 2 minutes. Stir in the tomato puree and gradually add the stock. Add the apple chutney, banana, raisins and salt and pepper to taste. Cover and microwave on Full Power for 12 minutes. Stir in the peeled prawns, chicken and lemon juice. Microwave on Full Power for 3-4 minutes.

Curried Prawns with Chicken (top left), Scampi Italienne (top right) and Plaice with Lemon (bottom).

Scampi Italienne

PREPARATION TIME: 10 minutes

MICROWAVE TIME: 10 minutes

SERVES: 4 people

½ red pepper, de-seeded and sliced
½ green pepper, de-seeded and sliced
50g (2oz) butter
1 small onion, finely chopped
1 clove garlic, crushed
150ml (¼ pint) dry white wine
15ml (1 tblsp) lemon juice
Salt and freshly ground black pepper
  to taste
450g (1lb) frozen shelled scampi,
  thawed

Garnish
Lemon butterflies
Savory

Put the red and green peppers, butter, onion and the garlic into a 1.75 litre (3 pint) casserole. Cover with the lid. Microwave on Full Power for 3 minutes. Stir in the white wine, lemon juice, salt and pepper to taste and the scampi. Cover and microwave on Full Power for 6-7 minutes, stirring once halfway through. Serve immediately, garnished with lemon butterflies and savory.

Special Fish Pie

PREPARATION TIME: 15 minutes

MICROWAVE TIME: 15 minutes

SERVES: 4 people

450g (1lb) young leeks, washed and
  cut into 4cm (1½ inch) lengths
4 large, firm tomatoes, skinned and
  sliced
10ml (2 tsp) mixed dried herbs
25g (1oz) butter
Salt and freshly ground black pepper
  to taste
350g (12oz) cod, skinned and filleted
30ml (2 tblsp) frozen sweetcorn
  kernels, thawed
50g (2oz) grated Cheddar cheese
15ml (1 tblsp) tomato sauce
450g (1lb) potatoes, peeled, cooked
  and mashed

Arrange the leeks and tomatoes in the base of a casserole dish; sprinkle with half the herbs. Dot the butter over the surface and season well with salt and pepper. Cover and microwave on Full Power for 5 minutes. Cut the fish into 2.5cm (1 inch) pieces. Arrange evenly over the vegetables and

season once again. Cover and microwave on Full Power for 7 minutes. Drain off excess liquid and add the sweetcorn. Add the cheese, tomato sauce and remaining herbs to the potato; beat well. Pile or pipe the potato on top of the fish and vegetables. Microwave, uncovered, on Full Power for about 3 minutes. Brown under a pre-heated grill, if desired, and serve immediately.

Mackerel with Apple Sauce

PREPARATION TIME: 30 minutes

MICROWAVE TIME: 15 minutes

SERVES: 4 people

4 fresh mackerel, heads and fins
  removed, and filleted (approx.
  175g (6oz) per fish)
100g (4oz) fresh brown breadcrumbs
1 eating apple, peeled, cored and
  chopped
50g (2oz) shredded suet
5ml (1 tsp) lemon juice
10ml (2 tsp) finely chopped fresh
  parsley
1 onion, peeled and finely chopped
Salt and freshly ground black pepper
  to taste
1 egg, beaten
30ml (2 tblsp) apple juice

Sauce
750g (1½lb) cooking and eating
  apples (mixed), peeled, cored and
  sliced
10ml (2 tsp) lemon juice
10ml (2 tsp) caster sugar
15g (½oz) butter

Put the breadcrumbs, apple, suet, lemon juice, parsley and onion into a mixing bowl. Season to taste with salt and pepper. Mix with the beaten egg to bind. Divide the stuffing amongst the fish, pressing it well into each cavity. Make an incision with a sharp knife in the thickest side of each fish. Arrange the fish, nose to tail, in a shallow dish. Pour over the apple juice. Cover tightly with cling film and pierce. Microwave on Full Power for 8 minutes. Stand on one side while preparing the sauce. Put the apples into a 1.75 litre (3 pint) Pyrex mixing bowl with the lemon juice and sugar. Cover. Microwave on Full Power for 6-7 minutes. Allow to stand for 3 minutes. Beat together with the butter and the juices from the cooked fish. Serve immediately with the fish.

Trout with Almonds

PREPARATION TIME: 10 minutes

MICROWAVE TIME: about 19 minutes

SERVES: 4 people

4 rainbow trout, cleaned and gutted
  (approx 225g (8oz) per fish)
65g (2½oz) butter
1 clove garlic, crushed
Salt and freshly ground black pepper
  to taste
250ml (8 fl oz) double cream
50g (2oz) flaked almonds

Garnish
Fresh parsley

Use a very small amount of foil to mask the tail of each fish. Make 2 incisions in the thick side of each fish. Put 50g (2oz) of the butter into a suitable shallow dish and microwave on Full Power for 1½ minutes. Stir the garlic and salt and pepper into the butter. Arrange the fish, nose to tail, in the flavoured butter. Cover with cling film and pierce. Microwave on Full Power for 8 minutes. Turn each fish over once during cooking. Stand aside, covered. Put the almonds and the remaining butter into a soup bowl. Microwave on Full Power for 2 minutes. Stir. Microwave on Full Power for a further 2 minutes. Pour the cream over the fish, and microwave on Power 4 or, Simmer, for 5 minutes. Serve immediately sprinkled with the toasted nuts and garnished with parsley.

Devilled Herrings

PREPARATION TIME: 15-20 minutes

MICROWAVE TIME: 6-7 minutes

SERVES: 4 people

30ml (2 tblsp) dry mustard
15ml (1 tblsp) brown sugar
15ml (1 tblsp) malt vinegar
4 fresh herrings, about 225g (8oz)
  each
75ml (⅛ pint) white wine
1 medium onion, finely chopped
15ml (1 tblsp) finely chopped fresh
  parsley
Salt and freshly ground black pepper
  to taste
25g (1oz) butter

Blend together the mustard, sugar and vinegar. Cut the heads and the tails off the fish and remove the back-bones; flatten each fish.

Spread the mustard mixture inside the herrings and roll up. Secure with cocktail sticks. Arrange the fish in a suitable dish. Add the wine, parsley and salt and pepper to taste. Dot with butter. Cover tightly with cling film or a lid. Pierce if using cling film. Microwave on Full Power for 6-7 minutes. Stand for 3 minutes before serving.

Smoked Haddock with Scrambled Eggs

PREPARATION TIME: 5-10 minutes

MICROWAVE TIME: 11 minutes

SERVES: 3-4 people

450g (1lb) smoked haddock fillet
Salt and freshly ground black pepper
  to taste
150ml (¼ pint) milk
50g (2oz) butter
4 eggs
15ml (1 tblsp) finely chopped fresh
  parsley

Arrange the fish in a shallow container. Season with salt and pepper and add 30ml (2 tblsp) of the milk. Dot the fish with half the butter. Cover with cling film and pierce. Microwave on Full Power for 7 minutes. Set aside, covered. Make the scrambled egg: beat the eggs with the remaining milk in a 1.75 litre (3 pint) mixing bowl; season to taste and add the remaining butter. Microwave on Full Power for 2 minutes; beat well, using a balloon whisk. Microwave on Full Power for 2 minutes until light and fluffy. Carefully arrange the fish on a serving dish. Spoon the scrambled eggs either side of the fish. Sprinkle with the chopped parsley and serve immediately.

Special Fish Pie (top), Mackerel with Apple Sauce (centre) and Trout with Almonds (bottom).

Prawns Creole

PREPARATION TIME: 15 minutes
MICROWAVE TIME: 18 minutes
SERVES: 4 people

225g (8oz) long grain rice
600ml (1 pint) boiling chicken stock
2 medium size onions, chopped
½ red pepper, de-seeded and chopped
½ green pepper, de-seeded and chopped

225g (8oz) peeled prawns
425g (15oz) can pineapple segments in natural juice, drained
25g (1oz) seedless raisins
Salt and freshly ground black pepper to taste

Put the rice into a 1.75-2.25 litre (3-4 pint) mixing bowl. Pour on the boiling stock. Cover tightly with cling film and pierce once in the centre. Microwave on Full Power for 12 minutes. Set aside, covered with a clean tea towel. Put the onion and red and green pepper into a 1.2 litre (2 pint) mixing bowl. Cover with cling film and pierce. Microwave on Full Power for 3 minutes. Stir. Fork up the rice after 10 minutes standing time, and add the onions, peppers, prawns, pineapple, raisins and salt and pepper. Cover with cling film and pierce. Microwave on Full Power for 3 minutes to reheat. Serve immediately.

Smoked Haddock with
Scrambled Eggs (below left),
Prawns Creole (below) and
Devilled Herrings (below
right).

Meat Dishes

Sausagemeat Stuffing

PREPARATION TIME: 15 minutes

MICROWAVE TIME: 10 minutes

SERVES: 4 people

450g (1lb) pork sausagemeat
85g (3¼oz) packet parsley and
  thyme stuffing mix
15ml (1 tblsp) tomato sauce
5ml (1 tsp) made mustard
1 small onion, finely chopped
Salt and freshly ground black pepper
  to taste
150ml (¼ pint) boiling water

Put the sausagemeat into a 1.75 litre (3 pint) mixing bowl. Add all the remaining ingredients. Leave to stand for 3 minutes. Knead together until well mixed. Using dampened hands, form the sausagemeat mixture into 20 balls. Arrange on a large roasting rack, or in a ring on a large circular dish, on 2 sheets of absorbent kitchen paper. Microwave on Power 7, or Roast, for 10 minutes.

Savoury Mince with Dumplings

PREPARATION TIME: 20 minutes

MICROWAVE TIME: 23 minutes

SERVES: 4 people

2 rashers streaky bacon, de-rinded
  and chopped
1 medium onion, chopped
½ green pepper, de-seeded and
  chopped
750g (1½lb) raw minced beef or
  pork
1 beef stock cube, crumbled
2.5ml (½ tsp) mixed dried herbs
150ml (¼ pint) water
5ml (1 tsp) chive mustard
Salt and freshly ground black pepper
  to taste
425g (15.9oz) can butter beans,
  drained

Dumplings
100g (4oz) self-raising flour
50g (2oz) suet
2.5ml (½ tsp) dried tarragon

Put the bacon, onion and pepper into a soup bowl. Cover with cling film and pierce. Microwave on Full Power for 2 minutes. Put the mince into a 1.75 litre (3 pint) casserole dish. Microwave on Full Power for 4 minutes. Break down with a fork and stir in the onion mixture, stock cube, herbs, water and mustard. Season well with salt and pepper. Microwave on Power 6, or Roast, for 12 minutes. Stir in the butter beans. Set aside. To prepare the dumplings: mix together the flour, suet and tarragon. Bind with sufficient cold water to make an elastic dough. Divide into 6 dumplings and arrange on top of the mince. Cover with a lid and microwave on Power 7 for 4-5 minutes. Stand for 3 minutes before serving.

Mixed Meat Loaf

PREPARATION TIME: 30 minutes

MICROWAVE TIME: 27 minutes

SERVES: 6-8 people

1 clove garlic
175g (6oz) lean streaky bacon, de-
  rinded
450g (1lb) raw minced beef
225g (8oz) raw minced pork
175g (6oz) lambs' liver, finely
  chopped
175g (6oz) back bacon, de-rinded
  and finely chopped
50g (2oz) shredded suet
50g (2oz) fresh brown breadcrumbs
2.5ml (½ tsp) dried oregano
2.5ml (½ tsp) mixed dried herbs
Salt and freshly ground black pepper
  to taste
45ml (3 tblsp) sherry
1 egg, beaten

Glaze
30ml (2 tblsp) apricot jam or
  marmalade, sieved
5ml (1 tsp) French mustard
2.5ml (½ tsp) Bovril

Rub a 1.75 litre (3 pint) plastic bread baker with the clove of garlic. Lay the streaky bacon in the bread baker to line the base and the sides. In a large mixing bowl, mix the minced beef with the pork, liver, back bacon, suet, breadcrumbs and herbs. Season to taste. Beat together the sherry and the egg; add to the mixture and bind together. Transfer to the prepared bread baker. Smooth the top. Cover and microwave on Power 6, or Roast, for 27 minutes. Turn the dish ½ a turn twice during this time. Allow to stand for 10 minutes. Pour off the excess fat and carefully unmould the loaf. Mix all ingredients together for the glaze and brush over the top and sides of the meat loaf. Delicious hot or cold.

Cheesey Beef Cobbler

PREPARATION TIME: 30 minutes

MICROWAVE TIME: 20 minutes

SERVES: 4 people

450g (1lb) raw minced beef
1 onion, chopped
225g (8oz) can tomatoes, chopped
1 beef stock cube, crumbled
15ml (1 tblsp) bottled brown sauce
Celery salt and freshly ground black
  pepper to taste
30ml (2 tblsp) frozen peas

Scone Topping
225g (8oz) self-raising flour, sieved
  with 2.5ml (½ tsp) baking powder
50g (2oz) margarine or butter, chilled
50g (2oz) grated Cheddar cheese
2.5ml (½ tsp) mixed dried herbs
1 egg, mixed with 90ml (6 tblsp)
  milk
5ml (1 tsp) Bovril

Put the minced meat and onion into an 18cm (7 inch) souffle dish. Cover and microwave on Full Power for 4 minutes. Stir well with a fork. Stir in the tomatoes, stock cube, brown sauce and celery salt and pepper. Cover and microwave on Power 7, or Roast, for 10 minutes. Stir in the peas and set aside. Put the flour and baking powder into a 1.75 litre (3 pint) mixing bowl. Rub in the margarine or butter. Mix in the cheese and herbs. Add the beaten egg and milk and mix to a soft dough. Knead lightly. Roll the dough out to a thickness of 1cm (½ inch). Using a 5cm (2 inch) pastry cutter, cut the dough into scones. Arrange the scones on top of the mince. Cook, uncovered, on Full Power for 6 minutes. Serve immediately.

Note: to improve the colour of the scones mix the Bovril with a little water and use to brush the scones prior to cooking.

Lamb Curry

PREPARATION TIME: 20 minutes

MICROWAVE TIME: about
                      45 minutes

SERVES: 4 people

2 carrots, peeled and chopped
1 medium onion, chopped
25g (1oz) butter
25g (1oz) plain flour
15-20ml (3-4 tsp) mild curry powder
450g (1lb) lamb fillet, cubed
450ml (¾ pint) boiling chicken stock
15ml (1 tblsp) desiccated coconut
25g (1oz) sultanas
1 medium sized eating apple, peeled,
  cored and chopped
1 peach, peeled, stoned and roughly
  chopped
15ml (1 tblsp) tomato puree
30ml (2 tblsp) lemon juice
Salt and freshly ground black pepper
  to taste

Preheat a large browning dish, without the lid, for 3 minutes on Full Power. Put the carrots, onion and butter into the preheated dish. Microwave on Full Power for 2 minutes, covered. Stir in the flour, curry powder and meat. Microwave on Full Power for 4 minutes. Gradually add the stock, stirring all the time. Stir in the coconut, sultanas, apple, peach, tomato puree, lemon juice and seasoning to taste. Cover and

Lamb Curry (top left), Savoury Mince with Dumplings (top right) and Mixed Meat Loaf (bottom).

microwave on Full Power for 7 minutes. Stir. Microwave on Power 4, Simmer or Defrost, for 30-35 minutes. Stir twice during this time. Serve immediately.

Pasta with Pork and Liver

PREPARATION TIME: 15 minutes
MICROWAVE TIME: 25 minutes
SERVES: 4 people

30ml (2 tblsp) oil
1 medium onion, sliced
350g (12oz) raw minced pork
100g (4oz) chicken livers, minced
100g (4oz) mushrooms, chopped
225g (8oz) can tomatoes, chopped
45ml (3 tblsp) sherry
Salt and freshly ground black pepper
    to taste
1 beef stock cube, crumbled

175g (6oz) dried pasta shells
Chopped fresh parsley

Heat the browning dish, without the lid, for 4-6 minutes on Full Power. Put half the oil, the onion and minced meats into the preheated dish. Stir well. Microwave on Full Power for 4 minutes. Stir in all the remaining

ingredients, apart from the pasta and the parsley. Cover with the lid and microwave on Full Power for 3 minutes. Stir. Microwave, covered, on Power 5, or Simmer, for 10 minutes. Allow to stand whilst preparing the pasta. To cook the pasta, place the remaining oil and the pasta into a 2.25-2.75 litre (4-5 pint) bowl. Add 1.75 litres (3 pints) water and 2.5ml (½ tsp) salt to the pasta. Cover and microwave on Full Power for 8 minutes. Allow to stand for 5 minutes. Drain the pasta and arrange on a serving dish. Spoon the meat sauce evenly over the pasta, and garnish with chopped parsley. Serve immediately.

Pasta with Pork and Liver (far left), Cheesey Beef Cobbler (below) and Sausagemeat Stuffing (below right).

Chicken Breasts in Garlic Cream Sauce

PREPARATION TIME: 10 minutes

MICROWAVE TIME: 17 minutes

SERVES: 4 people

50g (2oz) butter
1 clove garlic, crushed
1 medium onion, sliced
2 rashers bacon, de-rinded and chopped
50g (2oz) button mushrooms, sliced
2.5ml (½ tsp) dried basil
Salt and freshly ground black pepper to taste
4 chicken breasts, skinned and boned (about 150g (5oz) each)
300ml (½ pint) double cream

Garnish
Savory
Toasted flaked almonds

Melt the butter in a 1.75 litre (3 pint) casserole dish for 1-2 minutes on Full Power. Stir in the garlic, onion, bacon, mushrooms, basil and salt and pepper to taste. Cover and microwave on Full Power for 2 minutes. Arrange the chicken breasts on top of the vegetables. Cover and microwave on Power 7, or Roast, for 10 minutes. Season the cream and pour evenly over the top to coat. Microwave on Roast, or Power 7, for 3 minutes. Garnish with savory and almonds. Serve immediately.

Chicken Casserole

PREPARATION TIME: 15 minutes

MICROWAVE TIME: about 40 minutes

SERVES: 4 people

4 chicken portions, skinned (about 225g (8oz) each)
25g (1oz) butter
1 onion, finely chopped
2 stems celery, chopped
2 carrots, chopped
30ml (2 tblsp) drained canned sweetcorn kernels
10ml (2 tsp) cornflour
300ml (½ pint) chicken stock
Salt and paprika to taste

Put the butter into a 2.25 litre (4 pint) casserole dish. Microwave on Full Power for 1 minute. Stir in the onion, celery and carrots. Cover with a lid and microwave on Full Power for 3 minutes. Pour the stock into the casserole, and add salt to taste. Arrange the chicken pieces

on top of the vegetables, keeping the thickest part to the outside of the dish. Sprinkle each chicken piece with a little paprika. Microwave, covered, on Full Power for 4 minutes. Stir. Microwave on Power 4, Simmer or Defrost, for a further 30 minutes. Using a draining spoon, transfer the chicken to a warmed serving dish. Cover with a piece of foil and set aside. Cream the cornflour with a little water and stir into the casserole dish. Microwave on Full Power for 2-3 minutes, until boiling and thickened. Stir in the sweetcorn. Serve the chicken pieces with the vegetable sauce spooned over the top.

Sausage Suet Pudding

PREPARATION TIME: 30 minutes

MICROWAVE TIME: 21 minutes

SERVES: 4 people

Filling
225g (8oz) pork sausages, cut into 2.5cm (1 inch) pieces
225g (8oz) chicken livers, roughly chopped
25g (1oz) seasoned flour
15ml (1 tblsp) oil
1 medium onion, chopped
½ green pepper, de-seeded and chopped
300ml (½ pint) well flavoured boiling stock
Salt and freshly ground black pepper to taste

Suet Pastry
225g (8oz) self-raising flour
2.5ml (½ tsp) salt
5ml (1 tsp) baking powder
100g (4oz) finely grated (or shredded) suet
150ml (¼ pint) water

Toss the sausages and chicken livers in the seasoned flour. Put the oil into a 1.75 litre (3 pint) mixing bowl. Microwave on Full Power for 2 minutes. Stir in the onion and green pepper. Microwave on Full Power for 2 minutes. Stir the chicken livers and sausage into the onion. Cover and microwave on Power 8, or Roast, for 5 minutes. Carefully stir in the boiling stock and salt and pepper to taste. Microwave on Full Power for 2-3 minutes, until thickened. Stir and set aside while preparing the pastry. Sieve the flour, salt and baking powder into a bowl. Stir in the suet and mix to a soft dough with the water. Knead lightly. Roll out ⅔ of

the pastry and use to line a greased 900ml (1½ pint) boilable plastic pudding basin. Roll the remaining pastry into a circle. Fill the pastry-lined basin with the filling mixture. Dampen the pastry rim with cold water and top with the circle of pastry. Seal edges. Cut a small slit in the top to allow the steam to escape. Cover loosely with absorbent kitchen paper or cling film. Microwave on Power 7, or Roast, for 9 minutes. Stand for 5 minutes before serving.

Herby Roast Chicken

PREPARATION TIME: about 35 minutes

MICROWAVE TIME: about 36 minutes

SERVES: 6 people

75g (3oz) fresh brown breadcrumbs
50g (2oz) shredded suet
5ml (1 tsp) finely chopped fresh parsley
5ml (1 tsp) finely chopped fresh tarragon
1 eating apple, peeled, cored and chopped
5ml (1 tsp) lemon juice
Salt and freshly ground black pepper to taste
1 small onion, finely chopped
1 egg, beaten
1¾kg (4lb) chicken, giblets removed

Coating
50g (2oz) butter
10ml (2 tsp) chicken seasoning
5ml (1 tsp) paprika
2.5ml (½ tsp) mixed dried herbs

Garnish
Watercress

To make the stuffing, combine the breadcrumbs, suet, parsley, tarragon, apple, lemon juice and seasoning to taste. Put the onion into a small bowl and microwave on Full Power for 1 minute. Add the onion to the other ingredients. Bind together with the beaten egg.

**Chicken Casserole (top right),
Herby Roast Chicken (top left),
Chicken Breasts in Garlic
Cream Sauce (bottom right)
and Sausage Suet Pudding
(bottom left).**

Roasting Meats

TYPE OF MEAT	MICROWAVE POWER LEVEL	TIME PER 450g (1lb)	INTERNAL TEMPERATURE AFTER MICROWAVING	INTERNAL TEMPERATURE AFTER STANDING
Chops 1. Lamb	Power 7 or Roast Use pre-heated browning dish)	7-8 minutes	Turn the chops over once during cooking time.	
2. Pork	Power 7 or Roast (Use pre-heated browning dish)	9-10 minutes	Allow to stand for 5-10 minutes before serving.	
Beef (Boned & Rolled)	Power 7 or Roast	5-6 minutes *Rare* 7-8 minutes *Medium* 8-10 minutes *Well done*	57°C/130°F 65°C/150°F 70°C/160°F	62°C/140°F 70°C/160°F 78°C/170°F
Beef on the Bone	Power 7 or Roast	5 minutes *Rare* 6 minutes *Medium* 8 minutes *Well done*	57°C/130°F 65°C/150°F 70°C/160°F	62°C/140°F 70°C/160°F 78°C/170°F
Poultry (Unboned)	Full Power	7 minutes	85°C/185°F	94°C/190°F
Pork	Power 7 or Roast	10-11 minutes	82°C/180°F	85°C/185°F
Lamb	Power 7 or Roast	8-9 minutes	78°C/170°F	82°C/180°F

1. Have joints boned and rolled for best results.
2. Use a microwave meat thermostat to gauge when the meat should be removed from the microwave oven.
3. Any joint which is 1½kg (3lbs) or over will brown in the microwave oven, to increase the colouring, use a browning agent before cooking, or flash the meat under a pre-heated hot grill after standing time.
4. Turn the joint over once during the cooking time.
5. Use a microwave roasting rack, or an upturned saucer, placed in a suitable dish so as to allow the juices to drain.

Stuff the neck end of the bird with the stuffing. Truss. Weigh the stuffed bird and calculate the cooking time accordingly (7 minutes per 450g (1lb)). Use small amounts of foil to mask the wings and the stuffed area, to prevent overcooking. Arrange the chicken in a suitable roasting dish, on two upturned saucers, or on a microwave roasting rack. Melt the butter in the microwave for 1 minute on Full Power. Brush the butter all over the chicken. Combine the chicken seasoning, paprika and herbs together and sprinkle all over the chicken. Cover with a split roasta bag. Microwave on Full Power for the calculated time. Allow the chicken to stand, covered with a tent of foil, before serving. Garnish with watercress.

Devilled Pork Chops

PREPARATION TIME: 10 minutes
MICROWAVE TIME: 16 minutes
SERVES: 4 people

30ml (2 tblsp) oil
4 chump pork chops (about 175g (6oz) each)
100g (4oz) butter
15ml (1 tblsp) dry mustard
30ml (2 tblsp) fresh breadcrumbs
15ml (1 tblsp) soya sauce
10ml (2 tsp) Worcestershire sauce
15ml (1 tblsp) tomato chutney
Salt and paprika to taste

Preheat the browning dish (without the lid) for 4-7 minutes, according to size, on Full Power. Put the oil into the heated dish and microwave on Full Power for 1 minute. Put the 4 chops into the dish, pressing them down well. Microwave on Full Power for 2 minutes. Turn the chops over and microwave on Power 7, or Roast, for 10 minutes. Combine all the remaining ingredients in a mixing bowl. Spread over the partly cooked chops. Microwave on Power 7, or Roast, for a further 3 minutes.

Beef or Pork Burgers

PREPARATION TIME: 20 minutes
MICROWAVE TIME: 6-7 minutes
SERVES: 4 people

450g (1lb) raw minced beef or pork
1 small onion, finely chopped
50g (2oz) fresh breadcrumbs
1 stock cube, crumbled
2.5ml (½ tsp) dried parsley
Salt and freshly ground black pepper to taste
15ml (1 tblsp) tomato sauce
5ml (1 tsp) made mustard
2 eggs, beaten
4 baps

Mix the mince, onion and breadcrumbs together. Add the stock cube and all the other ingredients, apart from the baps.

Mix well. Divide the mixture into 4 and form into burgers. Arrange on a microwave roasting rack, or other suitable dish, in a ring. Microwave on Full Power for 6-7 minutes, turning each burger over once halfway through cooking time. Split the baps and fill with the burgers.

Glazed Leg of Lamb

PREPARATION TIME: 25 minutes
MICROWAVE TIME: about 50 minutes

SERVES: 6 people

1¾kg (4lb) leg of lamb
2-3 cloves peeled garlic, cut into thin strips
Salt and freshly ground black pepper to taste
30ml (2 tblsp) tomato sauce
5ml (1 tsp) dry mustard
5ml (1 tsp) brown sugar
2.5ml (½ tsp) mixed dried herbs

Devilled Pork Chops (top right), Beef or Pork Burgers (centre left) and Glazed Leg of Lamb (bottom).

Make incisions all over the joint with a sharp knife; push a strip of garlic into each one. Season with salt and pepper. Combine the tomato sauce, mustard, brown sugar and herbs, and spread evenly over the joint. Arrange the joint on a roasting rack. Cover with a roasta bag. Microwave for 12 minutes on Full Power. Turn the joint over and microwave on Power 4, or Simmer, for 30-40 minutes or until the meat thermometer registers 70°C (160°F). Remove the joint. Cover with a tent of foil and allow to stand for 15 minutes before serving.

Rolled Roast Rib of Beef

PREPARATION TIME: 18 minutes

MICROWAVE TIME: 30 minutes

SERVES: 6-8 people

1¾kg (4lb) piece rib of beef, boned and rolled
Salt and freshly ground black pepper to taste
15ml (1 tblsp) tomato sauce
5ml (1 tsp) soft brown sugar

Stand the joint on the microwave roasting rack, in a suitable dish, keeping the fat side of the meat underneath. Season with salt and pepper. Microwave for 7 minutes, on Full Power. Turn the joint over and microwave on Roast, or Power 7, for 21 minutes. Remove from the microwave. Cover loosely with a tent of foil and allow to stand for 15 minutes. Spread the tomato sauce and brown sugar all over the fat. Microwave on Full Power for 2 minutes. (Check temperatures with a microwave thermometer. See chart).

Barbecue Lamb Chops

PREPARATION TIME: 10 minutes, plus marinating time

MICROWAVE TIME: 16 minutes

SERVES: 6 people

Marinade
30ml (2 tblsp) wine vinegar
60ml (4 tblsp) pure orange juice
15ml (1 tblsp) tomato sauce
5ml (1 tsp) soft brown sugar
5ml (1 tsp) French mustard
2.5ml (½ tsp) dried tarragon
5ml (1 tsp) mild curry powder
Salt and freshly ground black pepper to taste
5ml (1 tsp) oil
6 chump chops, each about 150g (5oz)

Blend all the ingredients together for the marinade, apart from the oil. Lay the chops in a large shallow dish and pour over the marinade. Cover and chill for at least two hours. Turn the chops over in the marinade, once or twice. Preheat a large browning dish for 7 minutes on Full Power. Put the oil and the drained chops into the dish, pressing the chops against the hot dish. Microwave, uncovered, on Full Power for 5 minutes. Turn the chops over. Microwave on Roast, or Power 7, for 3-4 minutes. Serve immediately.

Shepherd's Pie

PREPARATION TIME: 30 minutes

MICROWAVE TIME: 38 minutes

SERVES: 4 people

15ml (1 tblsp) cooking oil
2 courgettes, thinly sliced
1 small onion, finely chopped
450g (1lb) raw lean minced beef
15ml (1 tblsp) plain flour
Salt and freshly ground black pepper to taste
15ml (1 tblsp) tomato puree
60ml (4 tblsp) water
1 beef stock cube, crumbled
900g (2lb) potatoes
90ml (6 tblsp) milk
1 egg
15g (½oz) butter
30ml (2 tblsp) Red Leicester cheese, grated

Preheat a small browning dish on Full Power for 3½ minutes (if using a large browning dish preheat on Full Power for 5 minutes). Add the oil, courgettes and onion, and stir. Cover with a lid and microwave on Full Power for 2 minutes. Add the meat and microwave on Full Power for 3 minutes, stirring once. Add the flour, salt and pepper to taste, tomato puree, water and stock cube. Stir well and cover. Microwave on Power 7, or Roast, for 12 minutes, stirring after the first 4 minutes. Remove from the microwave oven and leave to stand. Meanwhile prepare the potatoes. Peel and dice the potatoes. Put them into a roasta bag with 60ml (4 tblsp) of the milk. Put the bag into a 1.75 litre (3 pint) bowl. Secure with a rubber band and pierce once at the base. Microwave on Full Power for 17 minutes (turn the bag over once during this time). Stand, covered, for 5 minutes. Drain the potatoes and mash them together with the egg, remaining milk and the butter. Pile the potato onto the meat mixture and sprinkle with the

Rolled Roast Rib of Beef (top) and Barbecue Lamb Chops (left).

cheese. Microwave on Full Power for 3-4 minutes, until the cheese has melted and the pie is very hot. To speed this recipe up you can use reconstituted powdered potato.

Pork with Leeks and Grapes

PREPARATION TIME: 20 minutes

MICROWAVE TIME: 53 minutes

SERVES: 4-5 people

30ml (2 tblsp) oil
1 carrot, peeled and sliced
1 stick celery, chopped
225g (8oz) potato, peeled and diced
450g (1lb) young leeks, washed and sliced
750g (1½lb) boned shoulder of pork, cut into 2.5cm (1 inch) cubes
25g (1oz) plain flour
Salt and freshly ground black pepper to taste
½ pint well flavoured chicken stock
100g (4oz) seedless white grapes

Preheat the browning dish for 4 or 7 minutes, according to size. Add the oil, carrot, celery, potato and leeks to the heated dish. Cover with the lid. Microwave on Full Power for 4 minutes. Using a perforated spoon, transfer the vegetables to a dinner plate. Return the browning dish to the microwave, without the lid, for 1 minute on Full Power. Toss the meat in the flour and seasoning; stir into the dish, turning so that all sides come in contact with the hot skillet. Microwave, uncovered, for 3 minutes on Full Power. Stir in the drained vegetables, stock and extra seasoning to taste. Cover with the lid. Microwave, covered, on Power 5, or Simmer, for 40 minutes. Stir in the grapes and serve after a standing time of 5 minutes.

Turkey Fricassee

PREPARATION TIME: 20 minutes

MICROWAVE TIME: 12 minutes

SERVES: 4 people

25g (1oz) butter
25g (1oz) plain flour
300ml (½ pint) chicken or turkey stock
Salt and freshly ground black pepper to taste
100g (4oz) button mushrooms, sliced
½ red pepper, de-seeded and chopped

4 rashers streaky bacon, de-rinded and chopped
1 medium onion, chopped
350g (12oz) cooked turkey, chopped
100g (4oz) stuffed olives, halved
30ml (2 tblsp) single cream
1 egg yolk

To make the sauce: melt the butter in a 1 litre (1¾ pint) jug for 1 minute on Full Power. Stir in the flour to make a smooth paste. Gradually stir in the stock, mixing well. Season with salt and pepper. Microwave on Full Power for 2 minutes. Beat well with a balloon whisk. Microwave on Full Power for 2 minutes. Beat in the sliced mushrooms. Put the red pepper, bacon and onion into a 1.2 litre (2 pint) mixing bowl. Cover and microwave on Full Power for 2 minutes. Stir. Arrange the cooked turkey in a serving dish. Add the pepper mixture and most of the halved olives (reserve a few for decoration). Beat the cream and egg yolk into the sauce. Pour the sauce evenly over the vegetables and turkey. Cover with cling film and pierce. Microwave on Power 5 for 5 minutes. Allow to stand for 5 minutes before serving. Garnish with the remaining olives.

Stewed Steak with Garlic

PREPARATION TIME: 25 minutes

MICROWAVE TIME: about 1 hour 40 minutes

SERVES: 4 people

750g (1½lb) chuck steak, cubed
15ml (1 tblsp) seasoned flour
2 leeks, washed and sliced
1 medium onion, sliced
1 carrot, peeled and chopped
2 cloves garlic, crushed
30ml (2 tblsp) cooking oil
2 rashers streaky bacon, de-rinded and chopped
425g (15oz) can tomatoes, chopped
15ml (1 tblsp) tomato puree
Salt and freshly ground black pepper to taste
300ml (½ pint) well flavoured beef stock
2.5ml (½ tsp) dried parsley

Toss the meat in the seasoned flour. Put the leeks, onions, carrot and the garlic into a 1.2 litre (2 pint) dish. Cover and microwave on Full Power for 3 minutes. Stir and set aside. Preheat the large browning dish, without the lid, for

This page: Pork with Leeks and Grapes.

Facing page: Stewed Steak with Garlic (top), Shepherd's Pie (centre right) and Turkey Fricassee (bottom).

7 minutes on Full Power. Pour the oil into the dish and quickly stir in the bacon and the meat. Press the meat against the sides of the dish. Cover and microwave on Full Power for 4 minutes. Stir, and add all the remaining ingredients. Cover. Microwave on Full Power for 4 minutes, and then on Power 4, or Simmer, for 70 minutes. Stir once after the first 30 minutes. Stir, and allow to stand for 10 minutes before serving.

Sauces and Preserves

Basic Savoury White Sauce

PREPARATION TIME: 5 minutes
MICROWAVE TIME: 5 minutes
MAKES: 300ml (½ pint)

25g (1oz) butter
25g (1oz) plain flour
300ml (½ pint) milk or chicken stock
Salt and freshly ground black pepper
   to taste

Melt the butter in a 1 litre (1¾ pint) jug. Microwave on Full Power for 1 minute until very hot. Stir in the flour to form a roux. Gradually stir in all the milk or stock. Season to taste with salt and pepper. Microwave on Full Power for 2 minutes. Beat well with a balloon whisk. Microwave on Full Power for 2 minutes. Beat with a balloon whisk and serve.

Variations on Basic White Sauce

Cheese Sauce

Beat 50g (2oz) finely grated cheese and 5ml (1 tsp) made mustard into

Mushroom Sauce (above right),
Basic Savoury White Sauce
(far right) and Cheese Sauce
(right).

the finished sauce. The heat of the sauce will melt the cheese.

Mushroom Sauce
Beat 50g (2oz) finely chopped mushrooms into the prepared sauce. The heat of the sauce will cook the mushrooms.

Egg Sauce
Chop 1 hard-boiled egg (cooked conventionally). Beat into the prepared sauce.

Parsley Sauce
Beat 15ml (1 tblsp) chopped fresh parsley into the finished sauce.

Onion Sauce
Finely chop 1 medium sized peeled onion and put it into a bowl. Cover with cling film and pierce. Microwave on Full Power for 1-1½ minutes to soften. Beat the softened onion into the prepared sauce (the onion should be softened before the sauce is made).

Cranberry Sauce

PREPARATION TIME: 10 minutes

MICROWAVE TIME: 4 minutes

MAKES: about 400ml (⅔ pint)

1 orange
225g (8oz) frozen cranberries, defrosted
100g (4oz) granulated sugar

Finely grate the rind from the orange into a 1.2 litre (2 pint) mixing bowl. Squeeze the juice from the orange and make up to 150ml (¼ pint) with cold water. Put the cranberries, sugar, orange juice and water into the mixing bowl. Microwave on Full Power for 4 minutes. Stir once, halfway through cooking time. Stir and serve.

Custard Sauce

PREPARATION TIME: 5 minutes	
MICROWAVE TIME: 4 minutes	
MAKES: 600ml (1 pint)	

30ml (2 tblsp) custard powder
50g (2oz) granulated sugar
600ml (1 pint) milk
30ml (2 tblsp) single cream

Put the custard powder and the sugar into a 1.2 litre (2 pint) mixing bowl. Mix to a smooth cream with a little of the milk. Put the remaining milk into a 1 litre (1¾ pint) jug and microwave on Full Power for 2 minutes. Pour the hot milk onto the blended custard powder, stirring well. Pour the custard back into the jug and microwave on Full Power for 2 minutes. Beat well with a balloon whisk. Allow to cool slightly before beating in the cream. Serve hot or cold.

Chocolate Sauce

PREPARATION TIME: 5 minutes	
MICROWAVE TIME: 5 minutes	
MAKES: about 300ml (½ pint)	

25g (1oz) butter
15ml (1 tblsp) cocoa powder
300ml (½ pint) milk
15ml (1 tblsp) golden syrup

Melt the butter in a 1 litre (1¾ pint) jug for 1 minute on Full Power. Stir in the cocoa, mixing well. Gradually add the milk, stirring. Microwave on Full Power for 2 minutes. Beat well with a balloon whisk. Microwave on Full Power for 2 minutes. beat in the golden syrup. Serve immediately.

Beefy Tomato Sauce

PREPARATION TIME: 10 minutes	
COOKING TIME: 20 minutes	
MAKES: about 600ml (1 pint)	

50g (2oz) butter
2 medium sized onions, finely chopped
50g (2oz) plain flour
750ml (1¼ pint) hot beef stock
30ml (2 tblsp) tomato puree
15ml (1 tblsp) vinegar
5ml (1 tsp) French mustard
5ml (1 tsp) soft brown sugar
5ml (1 tsp) Worcestershire sauce
15ml (1 tblsp) tomato sauce
Salt and freshly ground black pepper to taste

Melt the butter in a really large jug or mixing bowl for 1-2 minutes on Full Power. Stir in the onion and microwave, uncovered, for 3 minutes on Full Power. Stir in the flour, mixing well. Gradually add the stock, stirring continuously. Mix the puree with the vinegar and add to the sauce together with the French mustard, sugar, Worcestershire sauce, tomato sauce and salt and pepper to taste. Microwave on Full Power for 10 minutes. Beat well twice during this time. Turn on to Power 4, or Simmer, and microwave for a further 5 minutes. Beat well. Serve with meat balls, meat loaf, etc.

St Clement's Sauce

PREPARATION TIME: 10 minutes	
MICROWAVE TIME: 3½ minutes	
MAKES: about 200ml (⅓ pint)	

45ml (3 tblsp) fine cut marmalade
Juice of 1 lemon
Juice of 1 orange
5ml (1 tsp) arrowroot

Put the marmalade and lemon and orange juices into a 1 litre (1¾ pint) jug. Microwave on Full Power for 1½ minutes. Stir well. Microwave on Full Power for 1 minute. Blend the arrowroot to a smooth paste with a little cold water. Stir into the jug. Microwave on Full Power for 30 seconds. Stir. Microwave on Full Power for a further 30 seconds. Stir and serve.

Plum Jam

PREPARATION TIME: 20 minutes	
MICROWAVE TIME: 1 hour	
MAKES: 1¼kg (2½lb)	

Juice of 1 orange
900g (2lb) plums, halved and stoned
900g (2lb) granulated sugar

Put the juice and the plums into a large microwave container. Cover and microwave on Full Power for 10 minutes. Stir in the sugar to dissolve. Cover and microwave on Power 6 for about 40 minutes, or until setting point is reached. Test for setting. Pot and label in the usual way.

Strawberry Jam

PREPARATION TIME: 20 minutes, plus chilling overnight	
COOKING TIME: 31 minutes	
MAKES: about 1¼kg (2½lb)	

900g (2lb) freshly picked strawberries, hulled
900g (2lb) granulated sugar

Place the hulled strawberries in a 2.75 litre (5 pint) microwave dish. Add the sugar and stir. Cover and leave overnight in the refrigerator. Stir well. Cover and microwave on Full Power for 7 minutes, until boiling point is reached. Microwave on Power 5, or Simmer, for 24 minutes, until setting point is reached. Test for setting. Pot and label in the usual way.

Green Tomato Chutney

PREPARATION TIME: 40 minutes	
MICROWAVE TIME: 1¾-2 hours	
MAKES: about 2¾kg (6lbs)	

2 medium onions, finely chopped
350ml (12 fl oz) malt vinegar
250ml (8 fl oz) wine vinegar
1 small stem celery, chopped
2.5ml (½ tsp) mustard seed
1¾kg (4lb) green tomatoes, washed and chopped
2 large Bramley cooking apples, peeled, cored and chopped
175g (6oz) seedless raisins
1 clove garlic, crushed
4 peppercorns, 2 cloves and 2 chillies (tied in muslin)
450g (1lb) soft brown sugar
Salt and freshly ground black pepper to taste

Put the onions into a 750g (1½lb) pudding basin. Microwave on Full Power for 2 minutes. Put half the vinegar, the celery, mustard seed, tomatoes, apples, raisins, garlic and onions into a very large bowl.

Parsley Sauce (top), Cranberry Sauce (centre left), Onion Sauce (centre right) and Egg Sauce (bottom).

Crush the muslin bag with a rolling pin and add to the bowl. Stir. Cover and microwave on Full Power for 10 minutes. Stir in the sugar to dissolve. Add the remaining vinegar and season with salt and pepper to taste. Microwave on Full Power for 20-30 minutes. Remove the lid and stir well.

Microwave on Full Power, uncovered, for about 75 minutes until the mixture reduces and thickens. Stir twice during this time. Ladle into clean jam jars. Seal and label when cool. The chutney should be kept in a cool dark place for 2 months to mature, before using.

This page: Strawberry Jam (top), Plum Jam (centre right) and Green Tomato Chutney (bottom).

Facing page: Chocolate Sauce (top), St Clement's Sauce (centre left), Beefy Tomato Sauce (centre right) and Custard Sauce (bottom).

Sweets

Pear Upside Down Pudding

PREPARATION TIME: 25 minutes

MICROWAVE TIME: 9 minutes

SERVES: 6 people

Oil and caster sugar
45ml (3 tblsp) golden syrup
425g (15oz) can pear halves, drained
5 glace cherries, halved and rinsed
Recipe quantity Victoria Sandwich
mixture (see recipe)

Grease an 18cm (7 inch) souffle dish with oil and sprinkle the base and sides lightly with caster sugar. Spread the golden syrup over the bottom. Make an attractive pattern over the base with the pears and the glace cherries. Spoon the Victoria Sandwich mixture into the prepared dish. Smooth the top. Microwave on Full Power for 9 minutes. Allow to stand for 7 minutes in the dish before carefully turning out. Serve warm with custard or cream.

Apple and Blackcurrant Flan

PREPARATION TIME: 30 minutes

MICROWAVE TIME: 37 minutes

SERVES: 6 people

Base
150g (5oz) plain flour
150g (5oz) wholemeal flour
Pinch of salt
50g (2oz) margarine
50g (2oz) lard
1 egg and 30ml (2 tblsp) cold water,
beaten   together

Filling
450g (1lb) Bramley cooking apples,
* peeled, cored and sliced*
225g (8oz) blackcurrants
50g (2oz) caster sugar
75g (3oz) ground almonds
25g (1oz) butter
2 egg yolks

Meringue
3 egg whites
175g (6oz) caster sugar
Glace cherries and angelica for
* decoration*

To make the pastry, sieve the flours and salt into a mixing bowl. Rub in the margarine and lard until the mixture resembles fine breadcrumbs. Mix to a dough with the egg and cold water. Knead the dough lightly. Roll out and use to line a 25cm (10 inch) fluted flan dish. Press up pastry to come ½cm (¼ inch) above the rim of the dish. Prick the sides and base with a fork. Refrigerate for 15 minutes. Using a single strip of foil, about 2.5cm (1 inch) wide, line the inside edge of the flan case. Place 2 sheets of absorbent kitchen paper in the base. Weigh down with a few baking beans. Microwave on Full Power for 6 minutes. Remove the foil, beans and absorbent paper.

This page: Mille Feuille (top), Apple Mousse (centre right) and Pear Upside Down Pudding (bottom).

Facing page: Chocolate Rice Krispie (top), Rhubarb Sunburst (centre right) and Creme Caramel (bottom).

Microwave on Full Power for 2-3 minutes. Set aside. Put the fruits into a 1.75 litre (3 pint) mixing bowl. Cover and microwave on Full Power for about 7-8 minutes, stirring once halfway through. Stir in sugar to dissolve and beat to a puree. Cool. Beat in the ground almonds, butter and egg yolk. Put the egg whites into a large, clean bowl and whisk until stiff and dry. Beat in the sugar, a little at a time, until a thick glossy meringue results. Spread the fruit mixture into the flan case. Pipe or spread the meringue mixture on top to cover completely. Put the flan into a pre-heated moderate oven, 180°C, 350°F, Gas Mark 4, for 15-20 minutes, until pale golden. Serve sprinkled with tiny pieces of cherry and angelica.

Mille Feuille

PREPARATION TIME: 15-20 minutes, plus cooling time

MICROWAVE TIME: 6 minutes

SERVES: 6 people

225g (8oz) puff pastry (you can use a small packet of frozen puff pastry)
225g (8oz) fresh strawberries
300ml (½ pint) double cream, whipped
25g (1oz) caster sugar
100g (4oz) icing sugar, sieved
Pink food colouring
25g (1oz) toasted flaked almonds

Roll the pastry out into a circle 20cm (8 inch) in diameter. Place on a large dinner plate and chill for 10 minutes. Microwave, uncovered, for 5-6 minutes, on Full Power. Turn the plate once halfway through the cooking time. Brown the top under a pre-heated hot grill for a few seconds, if required. Allow to cool completely. Hull strawberries and roughly chop them. Fold the strawberries into the cream with the caster sugar. Split the pastry horizontally into 3 layers and place the first layer on a serving dish. Spread thickly with strawberries and cream. Top with the second pastry layer and spread with more strawberries and cream. Add the final layer of pastry, browned side uppermost. Put the icing sugar into a basin. Add a few drops of pink food colouring and just enough boiling water to produce a smooth glacé icing. Ice the Mille Feuille using a teaspoon – see picture. Sprinkle with the cold, toasted almonds and serve immediately.

Creme Caramel

PREPARATION TIME: 15 minutes, plus chilling time

MICROWAVE TIME: 28 minutes

SERVES: 4 people

Caramel
175g (6oz) granulated sugar
120ml (4 fl oz) cold water

Custard
450ml (¾ pint) milk
4 eggs, lightly beaten
50g (2oz) caster sugar

To make the caramel, place the granulated sugar and water into a large Pyrex jug. Microwave on Full Power for 9-11 minutes, or until a golden caramel results. Swirl the caramel evenly around the inside of a suitable, lightly-greased 900ml (1½ pint) dish. Leave to set. Put the milk into a large, clean jug and microwave on Full Power for 2 minutes. Add the beaten eggs and caster sugar. Strain onto the set caramel. Cover with cling film and pierce. Stand the dish in a larger container, which will act as a water bath. Pour in sufficient boiling water to come halfway up the sides of the dish containing the creme caramel. Microwave on Power 5, or Simmer, for about 15 minutes or until the custard has set. Remove from the water bath. Carefully peel away the cling film and allow to cool. Chill until ready to serve. Turn out and serve very cold with whipped cream.

Apple Mousse

PREPARATION TIME: 20 minutes

MICROWAVE TIME: 7 minutes

SERVES: 6 people

750g (1½lb) Bramley cooking apples, peeled, cored and sliced
Juice of 1 lemon
3 cubes of lime jelly (from a packet jelly)
45ml (3 tblsp) caster sugar
200ml (⅓ pint) whipping cream
2 egg whites
1 red-skinned eating apple

Put the prepared cooking apples into a 1.75 litre (3 pint) casserole dish with half the lemon juice and the lime jelly. Cover with a lid and microwave on Full Power for about 7 minutes until the apples are pulpy (stir once during this time). Beat with a fork, beating in the sugar until melted. Set aside and allow to cool. Blend the cooled

apple in a food processor or liquidizer until smooth. Add the half-whipped cream and process together for a few seconds. Whisk the egg whites in a clean bowl until they stand in soft peaks. Transfer the apple mixture to a large, clean bowl and fold in the beaten egg whites gently. Turn into a serving dish. Decorate with slices of eating apple, which have been brushed with the remaining lemon juice to prevent discolouration.

Rhubarb Sunburst

PREPARATION TIME: 10 minutes, plus chilling time

MICROWAVE TIME: 6 minutes

SERVES: 4 people

450g (1lb) fresh young rhubarb, cut into 2.5cm (1 inch) pieces
Finely grated rind and juice of 1 orange
15ml (1 tblsp) apricot jam
6 canned apricot halves, chopped

Place the rhubarb, orange rind and juice, and the jam into a 900ml (1½ pint) mixing bowl. Cover and microwave on Full Power for 6 minutes. Stir. Set aside to cool, and then chill. Stir in the chopped apricots. Serve with natural yogurt, ice cream or whipped double cream.

Chocolate Pudding with Cherries

PREPARATION TIME: 10 minutes

MICROWAVE TIME: 8½ minutes

SERVES: 4-6 people

75g (3oz) softened butter
75g (3oz) soft brown sugar
75g (3oz) self-raising flour
25g (1oz) cocoa powder
2 eggs
30ml (2 tblsp) milk
425g (15oz) can cherry pie filling

Put all ingredients, apart from the cherry pie filling, into a mixing bowl. Beat with a wooden spoon for 1 minute. Spoon into a lightly greased 900ml (1½ pint) plastic pudding basin. Microwave on Full Power for 3½-4 minutes, until well risen and springy to the touch. Set aside. Empty the cherry pie filling into a bowl and microwave on Full Power for 3 minutes, stirring after 1½ minutes. Turn the sponge pudding onto a dinner plate. Spoon the hot cherry sauce over the top and serve immediately.

Chocolate Rice Krispie

PREPARATION TIME: 15 minutes, plus chilling time

COOKING TIME: 5 minutes

MAKES: 16-20 wedges

100g (4oz) margarine
50g (2oz) caster sugar
25g (1oz) cocoa powder
50g (2oz) golden syrup
100g (4oz) Rice Krispies

Lightly grease 2 x 20cm (8 inch) sandwich tins with a little of the margarine (these are not to be used in the microwave). Put the remaining margarine, cut into pieces, into a 1.75 litre (3 pint) mixing bowl with the caster sugar, cocoa powder and golden syrup. Microwave on Power 5 or Simmer for 4 minutes. Stir halfway through, and again at the end. Microwave on Full Power for a further 1 minute. Stir in the Rice Krispies, making sure that they are all coated with the chocolate mixture. Divide between the prepared tins and smooth level with a knife. Cool and then chill until set. Cut into finger wedges to serve. As an alternative, 50g (2oz) washed, seedless raisins may be stirred in with the Rice Krispies.

Apple Ginger Crisp

PREPARATION TIME: 15 minutes

MICROWAVE TIME: 9 minutes

SERVES: 4-6 people

450g (1lb) Bramley cooking apples peeled, cored and sliced
50g (2oz) demerara sugar
15ml (1 tblsp) orange juice
65g (2½oz) butter
225g (8oz) plain ginger biscuits, crushed
50g (2oz) flaked almonds

Place the apples, sugar and orange juice into a 1.5 litre (2½ pint) casserole dish. Cover and microwave on Full Power for 4-5 minutes. Stir and set aside. Put the butter into a 1.75 litre (3 pint) mixing bowl. Microwave on Power 7, or Roast, for about 2 minutes, until melted. Stir the biscuits and almonds into the melted butter. Mix well. Microwave on Full Power for 2 minutes. Stir well with a fork after 1 minute. Carefully spoon the biscuit crumble over the apples. Serve immediately with whipped cream or ice cream. This pudding can also be served cold.

Chocolate Pudding with Cherries (left), Apple Ginger Crisp (below left) and Apple and Blackcurrant Flan (bottom).

Tea Time Treats

Celebration Gateau

PREPARATION TIME: 40 minutes

MICROWAVE TIME: 14 minutes

MAKES: 1 gateau

Cake
Caster sugar and oil for preparing the dish
3 eggs
150g (5oz) self-raising flour
25g (1oz) cocoa powder
2.5ml (½ tsp) baking powder
175g (6oz) soft margarine
175g (6oz) caster sugar

Icing
225g (8oz) icing sugar, sieved
75g (3oz) butter
10ml (2 tsp) boiling water
5ml (1 tsp) liquid coffee essence
Few drops of vanilla essence

Decoration
1 packet sponge finger biscuits
175g (6oz) plain chocolate
1m 40cm (1½ yards) brown nylon ribbon, 2.5cm (1 inch) wide

Lightly grease a deep, 18cm (7 inch) diameter souffle dish with oil. Line the base with a circle of greaseproof paper and use a little caster sugar to dust the sides. Knock out any surplus. Put all the ingredients for the cake into a mixing bowl. Beat for 1 minute. Spoon into the prepared souffle dish and smooth the top. Microwave on Power 7, or Roast, for about 7 minutes, and then on Full Power for 2-3 minutes until the sponge has risen to the top of the souffle dish and is set. Allow to stand in the container for 10 minutes before turning out onto a clean tea towel which has been sprinkled with a little caster sugar. Cool completely.

To make the icing: gradually beat the sieved icing sugar into the butter, adding the boiling water. Take 15ml (1 tblsp) buttercream out of the bowl and beat the coffee essence into it. Beat the vanilla essence into the remaining butter cream. Cut the cake in half horizontally and sandwich together with some of the vanilla buttercream. Spread the vanilla buttercream around the sides and across the top of the cake. Pipe half

the cake with vanilla butter cream and the other half with the coffee buttercream. Arrange the prepared sponge fingers, like soldiers, around the edge of the cake – see picture. Tie brown ribbon around to finish the gateau.
To prepare the sponge fingers: measure 1 sponge finger against the cooked cake. Trim all the sponge fingers to the same size. Break the chocolate into a large mixing bowl and microwave on Power 4 for 3-4 minutes. Stir. Dip the rounded end of the sponge fingers into the melted chocolate to coat the top half of each one. Arrange on a tray and leave in a cool plac for 10-15 minutes to set.

Chocolate Icing

PREPARATION TIME: 5 minutes

MICROWAVE TIME: 2½ minutes

25g (1oz) soft margarine, chilled
22ml (1½ tblsp) cocoa powder, sieved
150g (5oz) icing sugar, sieved
30ml (2 tblsp) milk

Put the margarine and cocoa into a 1.2 litre (2 pint) bowl. Microwave on Power 5, or Simmer, for 2½ minutes, until the margarine has melted and is very hot. Stir once, halfway through. Beat in the icing sugar and the milk. Beat with a wooden spoon until thick and glossy. Use to coat the top and sides of the cake.

Collettes

PREPARATION TIME: 30 minutes

MICROWAVE TIME: 7½ minutes

MAKES: 12

175g (6oz) plain chocolate
50g (2oz) milk chocolate
60ml (tblspk double cream
15g (½oz) butter
10ml (2 tsp) brandy or coffee essence
36 paper sweet cases, separated into twelve groups of three cases

Break the plain chocolate into pieces and put into a 900ml (1½

pint) bowl. Microwave on Power 3, or Defrost, for 4-5 minutes. Stir. Using a small paint brush or teaspoon, coat the base and sides of each group of paper cases with the melted chocolate. Leave to set. Put the milk chocolate and the butter into a clean bowl. Microwave on Power 3, or Defrost, for 2-2½ minutes. Beat well for a few minutes. Beat in the brandy or coffee essence. Half whip the cream and fold into the milk chocolate mixture using a metal spoon. Chill until firm enough to pipe. Peel the paper cases away from the set chocolate and discard. Pipe rosettes of chocolate filling into the chocolate case. Serve immediately in new paper sweet cases.

Fruit and Almond Cake

PREPARATION TIME: 20 minutes

MICROWAVE TIME: 13-16 minutes

MAKES: 1 cake

Use the large Anchor Hocking ring mould, which should be lightly greased and coated with caster sugar.

175g (6oz) soft margarine
175g (6oz) soft brown sugar
2.5ml (½ tsp) liquid gravy browning
3 eggs, beaten
175g (6oz) self-raising flour
2-3 drops almond essence
25g (1oz) ground almonds
50g (2oz) seedless raisins
50g (2oz) glace cherries, washed and roughly chopped
30ml (2 tblsp) milk

Cream margarine and sugar until light and fluffy. Beat in the gravy browning and beaten eggs, a little at a time (add 15ml (1 tblsp) flour with each addition of egg to prevent curdling). Beat in the almond essence, ground almonds and milk. Fold in the remaining flour, and then the raisins and cherries. Place in the prepared ring mould and smooth the top. Microwave on Power 6, or Roast, for 12-14 minutes, and then on Full Power for 1-2 minutes until just set. Stand for 15 minutes, before turning out. When quite cold, the top may be sprinkled with a little sieved icing sugar.

Cheese and Paprika Scones

PREPARATION TIME: 20 minutes

MICROWAVE TIME: 5-6 minutes

MAKES: about 10

225g (8oz) self-raising flour
Pinch salt
Pinch paprika
50g (2oz) firm margarine
50g (2oz) Red Leicester cheese, grated
5ml (1 tsp) made mustard
1 egg
45ml (3 tblsp) milk
5ml (1 tsp) Bovril

Sieve the flour, salt and paprika into a 1.75 litre (3 pint) mixing bowl. Rub in the margarine and fork in the cheese. Beat the mustard and egg together and mix with the milk. Mix into the dry ingredients, using a round bladed knife, to form a soft dough. Knead on a lightly floured board. Roll out to a thickness of 1cm (½ inch). Cut into 6cm (2½ inch) rounds. Arrange the shaped scones in a ring on a non-metallic tray, leaving a gap in the centre. Mix 5ml (1 tsp) Bovril with a little boiling water and brush over the surface of the scones (do not cover). Microwave immediately on Power 7, or Roast, for 5-6 minutes. Transfer to a cooling rack and allow to stand for 2-3 minutes. Serve hot with butter, or cold if preferred. As an alternative to the Bovril glaze, the cooked scones may be flashed under a pre-heated hot grill to brown and crisp them.

Celebration Gateau (top), Collettes (centre left) and Fruit and Almond Cake (bottom).

Microwave Meringues (right),
Victoria Sandwich (below) and
Porridge (bottom right).

Porridge

PREPARATION TIME: 5 minutes

MICROWAVE TIME: 9 minutes

SERVES: 3 people

2 cups milk and water, mixed
2.5ml (½ tsp) salt
1 cup porridge oats
75g (3oz) demerara sugar
75g (3oz) butter

Put the milk, water and salt into a 1.75 litre (3 pint) mixing bowl. Stir in the porridge oats. Microwave on Full Power for 3 minutes. Stir. Microwave on Full Power for 3 minutes. Stir. Microwave on Full Power for 3 minutes. Turn into individual serving dishes. Sprinkle with the brown sugar and top with the butter. Serve immediately.

Microwave Meringues

PREPARATION TIME: 20 minutes

MICROWAVE TIME: about 8 minutes

MAKES: 10 sandwiched meringues

1 egg white
180ml (12 tblsp) icing sugar, sieved
Pink food colouring
175g (6oz) chocolate buttercream
Chocolate Vermicelli

Put the egg white into a 1.75 litre (3 pint) mixing bowl and beat until frothy. Gradually work in the icing sugar and mix to give a really stiff fondant. Divide the fondant into two portions. Knead a few drops pink food colouring into one portion of fondant. Roll both the fondants separately into small balls, each about the size of a marble. Arrange 4 balls of fondant in a ring on a large dinner plate. Microwave on Full Power for 1½ minutes. Allow to stand for 2 minutes before removing to a cooling tray. Repeat until all the mixture has

been cooked. Fill the cooled meringue halves with the chocolate buttercream. Sprinkle with a little vermicelli and serve in paper cake cases.

Victoria Sandwich

PREPARATION TIME: 15 minutes

MICROWAVE TIME: 7 minutes

MAKES: 1 cake

Oil
Caster sugar for dusting
3 eggs
175g (6oz) self-raising flour
175g (6oz) soft margarine
175g (6oz) caster sugar
2 drops liquid gravy browning
30ml (2 tblsp) milk
45ml (3 tblsp) strawberry jam

Lightly grease an 18cm (7 inch) souffle dish with oil; dust the sides with a little caster sugar. Place a circle of greaseproof paper in the base. Put the eggs, flour, margarine, caster sugar, gravy browning and milk into a mixing bowl. Beat for 1 minute. spoon into the prepared dish and smooth the top. Microwave on Full Power for about 7 minutes. Test by putting a wooden cocktail stick into the centre of the sponge after a 3 minute standing time. The cocktail stick should come out clean. Stand for 10 minutes. turn out into a wire cooling rack. When quite cold, split in half horizontally. Sandwich together with the jam. Serve with a little caster sugar sprinkled over the top.

Cream Slices

PREPARATION TIME: 15-20 minutes, plus cooling time

MICROWAVE TIME: 6-8 minutes

MAKES: about 6 slices

225g (8oz) puff pastry (small packet frozen puff pastry can be used)
Black cherry jam
45ml (3 tblsp) icing sugar, sieved
A few drops of pink food colouring

Roll the pastry into an oblong about 10cm (4 inch) wide and 30-35cm (12-14 inches) long. Cut in half, crossways. Dampen the surface of a suitable container. Lift one half of the pastry onto the prepared tray and microwave on Full Power for 3-4 minutes, until well puffed up (when the door is

Roast, for 6-7 minutes. The sponge should be well risen and just 'set'. Remove from the microwave oven and allow to stand for 5 minutes before turning out. Allow to become quite cold. To make the buttercream, mix the cocoa with 30ml (2 tblsp) boiling water to form a smooth paste. Beat with the butter and icing sugar until light and creamy. Split the cooled cake in half horizontally. Sandwich together with a little of the butter-cream and arrange on a cake board. Use the remaining buttercream to completely coat the 'hedgehog'. Form a 'snout' for his nose. Fork all over. Cut most of the chocolate buttons in half and stud the hedgehog with these to represent the prickles. Use 1 whole chocolate button for his nose and 2 raisins for his eyes. Spread some green coconut around the base for grass.

Rich Fruit Cake

PREPARATION TIME: 30 minutes	
MICROWAVE TIME: 40 minutes	
MAKES: 1 cake	

100g (4oz) soft margarine
100g (4oz) dark soft brown sugar
30ml (2 tblsp) black treacle
5ml (1 tsp) gravy browning
3 eggs
45ml (3 tblsp) milk
225g (8oz) self-raising flour, sieved
   with 5ml (1 tsp) mixed spice and a
   pinch of salt
500g (1lb 2oz) mixed dried fruit
   (sultanas, raisins, currants and
   peel)
25g (1oz) chopped blanched almonds
50g (2oz) glace cherries, washed and
   quartered
45ml (3 tblsp) sherry or brandy

Lightly grease a deep, 23cm (9 inch) diameter souffle dish. Line the base with a circle of ungreased greaseproof paper and dust the

opened, the pastry should hold its shape). Allow to stand for 2-3 minutes and then remove to a cooling tray. Repeat the process with the remaining half of the pastry. Allow to cool. Using a sharp knife, divide each layer into 3 slices. Sandwich each group of three layers together with the jam. Mix the icing sugar with a little boiling water to make a smooth, glossy icing. beat in a few drops pink food colouring. Quickly spread the icing over the top of each layered slice. Cut each one into 3 slices.

Mr Hedgehog Cake

PREPARATION TIME: 40 minutes	
MICROWAVE TIME: 3½-7 minutes	
MAKES: 1 cake	

75g (3oz) softened margarine
75g (3oz) caster sugar
100g (4oz) self-raising flour
2 eggs
15ml (1 tblsp) milk
15ml (1 tblsp) cocoa powder
100g (4oz) butter
225g (8oz) icing sugar, sieved
1 packet chocolate buttons
2 raisins
Green coloured coconut for grass

To make the sponge, put the margarine, the caster sugar, flour, eggs and milk into a mixing bowl. Beat with a wooden spoon for 1 minute. Lightly grease the base and sides of a 900ml (1½ pint) Pyrex or plastic pudding basin. Fill with the sponge mixture and smooth the top. Microwave on Full Power for 3½ minutes, or on Power 6, or

This page: Mr Hedgehog Cake (top), Cream Slice (centre left) and Rich Fruit Cake (bottom).

Facing page: Pineapple Gateau (top right), Chocolate Pear Sponge (centre left) and Cheese and Paprika Scones (bottom).

sides with a little caster sugar (knocking out any surplus). Beat the margarine, sugar, treacle and gravy browning in a large mixing bowl until light and fluffy. Gradually beat in the eggs and the milk. Add 15ml (1 tblsp) flour with each addition of egg, to prevent it curdling. Fold in the remaining flour using a metal spoon. Fold in the fruits, nuts and glace cherries, together with the sherry or brandy. Spoon the mixture into the prepared container. Microwave on Power 4, Simmer or Defrost, for 40 minutes. Remove from the microwave oven and allow to stand in its dish for 20 minutes before turning out. When quite cold, the cake may be marzipanned and iced, or finished with glace fruits, and glazed. Allow the cake to mature for at least 1 month before using.

Date and Walnut Loaf Cake (below) and Crepes Suzette (bottom).

Crepes Suzette

PREPARATION TIME: 25 minutes

MICROWAVE TIME: about 24 minutes

SERVES: 4-6 people

Pancakes
120g (4oz) plain flour
Pinch salt
1 egg
150ml (¼ pint) milk
150ml (¼ pint) water
Cooking oil

Sauce
75g (3oz) butter
50g (2oz) caster sugar
Grated rind of 1 orange
Grated rind and juice of ½ a lemon
60ml (4 tblsp) brandy or Cointreau

Sieve the flour and salt into a bowl. Make a well in the centre. Add the egg and half of the milk. Beat well. Gradually beat in the remaining milk and the water. Beat in 5ml (1 tsp) oil. Allow to stand for 10 minutes. Fry the pancakes in the usual way, making 12 pancakes in all. Fold the 12 cooked pancakes in half and then in half again, to form triangles. Arrange in a shallow dish. To make the sauce, put the butter into a 1 litre (1¾ pint) jug and microwave on Defrost for 5 minutes, or until melted and hot. Stir in the sugar to dissolve. Add the fruit rinds, lemon juice, and the brandy or Cointreau. Microwave on Full Power for 2 minutes. Stir. Pour over the pancakes. Cover with cling film and microwave on Power 5, or Simmer, for 5 minutes. Turn each pancake over in the sauce before serving. Serve piping hot.

Pineapple Gateau

PREPARATION TIME: 30 minutes

MICROWAVE TIME: 7 minutes

MAKES: 1 gateau

Oil and caster sugar
1 recipe quantity Victoria Sandwich
  mixture (see recipe)
225g (8oz) can pineapple slices,
  drained
300ml (½ pint) whipping cream,
  whipped
100g (4oz) chopped blanched
  almonds, toasted
Angelica for decoration

Lightly grease an 18cm (7 inch) souffle dish or plastic pan with oil. Put a circle of greaseproof paper into the base of the dish; dust the base and sides with caster sugar (knock out any surplus). Spoon the prepared Victoria Sandwich mixture into the dish, and smooth the surface. Microwave on Full Power for about 7 minutes. Allow to stand for 10 minutes before turning out onto a wire cooling rack. Once the cake is quite cold, remove the greaseproof paper. Split the cake in half horizontally. Chop 1 slice of pineapple and mix with 45ml (3 tblsp) of the whipped cream; use to sandwich the cake layers together. Spread some of the cream round the sides of the cake and roll it in nuts to coat evenly. Arrange on a serving dish. Spread the top with the remaining cream, piping it if liked. Decorate the top with pineapple and angelica – see picture.

Chocolate Pear Sponge

PREPARATION TIME: 15 minutes

MICROWAVE TIME: 6 minutes

MAKES: 1 sponge cake

90g (3½oz) self-raising flour
15g (½oz) cocoa powder
2.5ml (½ tsp) baking powder
100g (4oz) soft margarine
15ml (1 tblsp) milk
5ml (1 tsp) mixed spice
100g (4oz) ripe pear, peeled, cored
  and chopped
Oil and caster sugar for preparing the
  souffle dish

Put all the ingredients, apart from the pear, into a 1.75 litre (3 pint) mixing bowl. Mix with a wooden spoon and then beat for 1 minute. Fold in the pear, using a metal spoon. Lightly grease an 18cm (7 inch) souffle dish; line the base with a circle of greaseproof paper and coat the sides with a little caster sugar. Turn the mixture into the prepared souffle dish and smooth the top. Microwave on Power 6, or Roast, for 4 minutes, and them on Full Power for 2 minutes. Allow to stand for 10 minutes before turning out onto a cooling rack. The cooling rack should be covered with a clean tea towel, sprinkled with a little caster sugar. When quite cold, ice the cake with chocolate icing.

Date and Walnut Loaf Cake

PREPARATION TIME: 15 minutes

COOKING TIME: 6 minutes

MAKES: 1 loaf

2 eggs
60ml (4 tblsp) milk
15ml (1 tblsp) golden syrup
5ml (1 tsp) gravy browning
100g (4oz) soft margarine
175g (6oz) self-raising flour
75g (3oz) soft brown sugar
75g (3oz) chopped stoned dates
1 small banana, sliced
50g (2oz) walnuts, chopped

Put the eggs, milk, syrup, gravy browning, margarine, flour and brown sugar into a large mixing bowl. Beat with a wooden spoon. Using a metal spoon, fold in the dates, banana and walnuts. Turn into a lightly greased 1.75 litre (3 pint) microwave bread baker. Microwave on Full Power for about 6 minutes, turning the dish a half turn, halfway through cooking time. Allow to stand in the bread baker for 10 minutes before turning out. Serve sprinkled with caster sugar

Index

Dep. Leg. 9-11.017-